Jordan

Travel Guide

2025

Your travel companion to having a
memorable stay while touring this
destination.

Ashton Z. Bennett

TABLE OF CONTENT

Introduction:

Overview of Jordan

Historical Significance

Jordan's history is a mosaic of human civilization, dating back to prehistoric times. The region has been inhabited by numerous civilizations, including the Ammonites, Moabites, and Edomites, whose remnants can still be found today. However, it is perhaps best known for its association with the Nabataeans, an ancient Arab people who established the city of Petra around the 6th century BC. This city, carved into rose-red sandstone cliffs, is now one of the New Seven Wonders of the World and a UNESCO World Heritage site. Petra is located in the southwestern desert, and exploring its intricacies is like stepping back in time.

Jordan was also a significant part of the Roman Empire. The ruins of Jerash, also known as the ancient city of Gerasa, provide a glimpse into this period. Located 48 kilometers north of Amman, Jerash boasts well-preserved Roman architecture, including the impressive Hadrian's Arch, the Corinthian columns of the Temple of Artemis, and a vast oval plaza.

Modern Day Jordan

Today, Jordan is a modern, vibrant nation with a population of around 10 million people. The capital city, Amman, is a bustling metropolis where ancient meets contemporary. It is a city of contrasts, with its modern buildings, upscale restaurants, and shopping centers juxtaposed against historical sites such as the Citadel and the Roman Theater. The Citadel, located on Jabal al-Qal'a, one of the seven hills that originally made up Amman, offers panoramic views of the city and houses important archaeological artifacts in the Jordan Archaeological Museum.

Amman serves as a gateway to exploring the rest of the country. From here, you can easily access various regions, each with its unique attractions. For instance, a few hours south of Amman lies the Dead

Sea, the lowest point on earth, where you can float effortlessly in the salty waters and enjoy the therapeutic mud. To the north, the lush Jordan Valley, part of the Great Rift Valley, contrasts sharply with the arid deserts to the east and south.

Cultural Heritage

Jordan's cultural heritage is as rich and varied as its history. The country is predominantly Arab, with a significant Bedouin population. Bedouin culture is an integral part of Jordanian identity, and you can experience their traditional hospitality in places like Wadi Rum. Known as the Valley of the Moon, Wadi Rum is a protected desert wilderness in southern Jordan. The dramatic landscape, with its towering sandstone mountains and vast, echoing emptiness, has been the backdrop for many films, including "Lawrence of Arabia."

In Wadi Rum, you can stay in Bedouin-style camps, enjoy traditional meals, and explore the desert on camelback or in a 4x4 vehicle. The clear night skies offer spectacular stargazing opportunities, and spending a night under the stars is an unforgettable experience.

Cuisine

Jordanian cuisine is a delightful fusion of flavors and ingredients. Influenced by its geographical neighbors, it features a mix of Mediterranean, Middle Eastern, and Bedouin traditions. One of the most famous dishes is mansaf, the national dish, which consists of lamb cooked in a sauce of fermented dried yogurt and served with rice or bulgur. Another popular dish is makloubeh, a savory upside-down rice cake with meat and vegetables.

Amman, with its diverse food scene, offers a range of dining options, from street food stalls to high-end restaurants. For an authentic culinary experience, visit Hashem Restaurant in downtown Amman, renowned for its delicious falafel, hummus, and fuul (fava bean dip). Another must-visit is Sufra Restaurant, located on Rainbow Street, where you can enjoy traditional Jordanian dishes in a charming setting.

Natural Wonders

Jordan is home to a variety of natural wonders, each offering unique experiences. The Dead Sea, located at 430 meters below sea level, is known for its high salinity and mineral-rich mud, which are believed to have therapeutic properties. The surrounding area also boasts luxury resorts and spas, such as the Kempinski Hotel Ishtar Dead Sea, where you can indulge in a range of wellness treatments.

Another natural gem is the Dana Biosphere Reserve, Jordan's largest nature reserve. Spanning over 320 square kilometers, it encompasses diverse landscapes, from oak and juniper forests to desert plains. The reserve is a haven for wildlife, including the endangered Nubian ibex and the Syrian serin. Hiking in Dana offers an opportunity to connect with nature and enjoy the stunning scenery.

Religious Significance

Jordan is a significant destination for religious tourism, attracting pilgrims from around the world. It is home to several sites mentioned in the Bible, making it an important destination for Christians. Mount Nebo, located about 10 kilometers northwest of Madaba, is believed to be the place where Moses viewed the Promised Land before his death. The site offers breathtaking views of the Jordan Valley and the Dead Sea, and you can visit the Memorial Church of Moses, which houses ancient mosaics.

Another important religious site is the Baptism Site of Jesus Christ, also known as Bethany Beyond the Jordan. Located on the east bank of the Jordan River, it is believed to be the place where John the Baptist baptized Jesus. The site has been recognized by the Vatican and UNESCO, and you can explore the archaeological remains and visit the nearby churches.

Safety and Hospitality

Jordan is known for its safety and the hospitality of its people. Despite being in a region often associated with conflict, Jordan has remained a stable and peaceful country. The government places a high priority on the safety of tourists, and you will find the locals to be welcoming and friendly. Jordanians take pride in their tradition of hospitality, and it is common to be invited for tea or a meal by strangers.

When traveling in Jordan, it is important to respect local customs and traditions. Dress modestly, especially when visiting religious sites, and be mindful of the conservative nature of Jordanian society. English is widely spoken, particularly in tourist areas, making communication relatively easy.

Brief History and Cultural Background

Brief History of Jordan
Jordan's history is one of the oldest and most intriguing in the world. The region, which encompasses the modern-day Kingdom of Jordan, has been inhabited since the Paleolithic era. Over thousands of years, it has seen the rise and fall of many civilizations, each leaving its mark on the land.

Ancient Civilizations
The earliest known inhabitants of Jordan were nomadic tribes. Around 8,000 BCE, these nomads began settling in agricultural communities, leading to the development of some of the world's first cities. The city of Jerash, known as Gerasa in antiquity, is one of the best-preserved Roman provincial towns in the world. Walking through Jerash's colonnaded streets, you can almost hear the echoes of the past, from bustling markets to chariot races in the hippodrome.

The Nabateans, an Arab people who settled in southern Jordan over 2,000 years ago, are perhaps the most famous of Jordan's ancient inhabitants. They established a vast trading network and built the city of Petra, now a UNESCO World Heritage Site. Petra, with its rock-cut architecture and water conduit system, stands as a testament to the ingenuity and skill of the Nabateans. The iconic Treasury (Al-Khazneh) and the Monastery (Ad-Deir) are must-see highlights for any visitor.

Roman and Byzantine Periods
After the Nabateans, Jordan became part of the Roman Empire. During this period, many cities flourished, including Jerash and Amman, then

known as Philadelphia. The Romans left behind a wealth of architectural marvels, including temples, theatres, and colonnaded streets. The city of Jerash is often referred to as the "Pompeii of the East" due to its remarkable state of preservation.

The Byzantine era brought the spread of Christianity, leading to the construction of numerous churches and mosaics. The town of Madaba is particularly famous for its Byzantine mosaics, including the 6th-century mosaic map of the Holy Land in St. George's Church. This map, made from over two million pieces of colored stone, provides valuable insights into the region's geography during the Byzantine period.

Islamic Period
In the 7th century, Jordan became part of the rapidly expanding Islamic Empire. The Umayyad dynasty, the first great Muslim dynasty, left significant architectural and cultural influences in the region. One of the most notable examples is the desert castles scattered throughout the eastern desert, such as Qasr Amra, a UNESCO World Heritage Site renowned for its early Islamic art and architecture.

Amman, known as Philadelphia during the Roman period, was re-established as the capital of the region under the Umayyads. The Citadel of Amman, with its ancient ruins and panoramic views of the city, offers a glimpse into this era. The Citadel includes the Umayyad Palace and the remains of a Byzantine church, illustrating the continuity of occupation and cultural layering over centuries.

Cultural Background
Jordan's culture is a unique blend of traditional Bedouin life and modern urban development. The Bedouin, traditionally nomadic desert dwellers, have significantly influenced Jordanian culture. Their values of hospitality, honor, and loyalty remain central to Jordanian society.

Bedouin Traditions
Hospitality is a cornerstone of Bedouin culture. Visitors are often welcomed with coffee and dates, and it is customary to share stories and meals. The Bedouins are renowned for their storytelling, passing down tales of heroism, love, and adventure through generations. While in

Jordan, you may have the opportunity to experience this hospitality firsthand, especially if you visit Wadi Rum or Petra, where many Bedouin families still live and work.

Language and Religion
Arabic is the official language of Jordan, and you will hear it spoken everywhere, from the markets of Amman to the villages in the Jordan Valley. English is widely understood, especially in tourist areas, making travel relatively easy for English-speaking visitors.

Islam is the predominant religion, and it plays a significant role in daily life. The call to prayer from mosques is a familiar sound, and Fridays are observed as the holy day. However, Jordan is known for its religious tolerance and is home to several Christian communities. This religious diversity is particularly evident in cities like Madaba and Amman, where churches and mosques coexist peacefully.

Modern Jordan
Today, Jordan is a modern, progressive country that balances its rich heritage with contemporary influences. The capital city, Amman, is a vibrant metropolis with a thriving arts scene, bustling markets, and diverse dining options. It is a city where ancient ruins stand alongside modern skyscrapers, reflecting Jordan's unique ability to honor its past while embracing the future.

Personal Stories
To truly understand Jordan, you must immerse yourself in its stories. Imagine sitting in a Bedouin tent in Wadi Rum, sipping sweet tea as your host recounts tales of life in the desert. Picture yourself walking through the ancient streets of Petra, feeling the weight of history in every step. Visualize exploring the Roman ruins of Jerash, where the grandeur of a bygone era comes to life before your eyes.

One traveler, Sarah, recalls her visit to Petra: "As I walked through the Siq, the narrow gorge leading to Petra, I felt like I was stepping back in time. When the Treasury finally came into view, it was more magnificent than I had ever imagined. The intricate carvings on the rose-red stone were breathtaking. It was a moment of awe that I will never forget."

Another visitor, Ahmed, shares his experience in Amman: "The Citadel of Amman was a highlight of my trip. Standing on the ancient hilltop, I could see the layers of history all around me. From the Roman temple to the Umayyad palace, it was a journey through time. The view of the modern city below was a stark contrast, reminding me of Jordan's rich past and dynamic present."

These personal stories, woven into the fabric of Jordan's history and culture, create a tapestry that is as compelling as the landscape itself. Jordan is not just a destination; it is a journey through time, a land where the past and present coexist in a harmony that captivates and enchants every visitor.

Geography and Climate

Geography

Jordan is strategically positioned in the Middle East, bordered by Saudi Arabia to the south and east, Iraq to the northeast, Syria to the north, Israel, and the Palestinian territories to the west, and the Red Sea to the southwest. The country spans an area of approximately 89,342 square kilometers (34,495 square miles), making it slightly smaller than Portugal.

One of the most defining features of Jordan's geography is the Great Rift Valley, which runs through the western part of the country. This geological wonder includes the Jordan River, the Dead Sea, and the Wadi Araba desert valley. The Jordan River, an essential water source and historical landmark, flows into the Dead Sea, the lowest point on Earth at 430 meters (1,411 feet) below sea level. The Dead Sea is renowned for its high salinity, allowing you to float effortlessly on its surface.

To the east of the Jordan River lies the East Bank, a plateau that gradually rises from the Jordan Valley and extends into the desert. This area includes the capital city, Amman, which sits at an elevation of about 850 meters (2,789 feet) above sea level. Amman is a bustling metropolis that seamlessly blends modernity with its rich historical heritage.

The southern part of Jordan is dominated by the arid desert landscapes of the Arabian Desert, also known as the Eastern Desert. This region is sparsely populated and characterized by vast stretches of sand dunes, rocky outcrops, and ancient trade routes. The Wadi Rum desert, often referred to as the Valley of the Moon, is a particularly stunning part of this landscape, famous for its red sandstone mountains and dramatic rock formations.

In contrast, the western region of Jordan is more fertile, with the Jordan Valley and the highlands offering lush agricultural lands. The highlands, which include cities like Ajloun and Irbid, are covered with forests of oak and pine, providing a cooler and greener environment compared to the surrounding deserts.

Climate

Jordan's climate varies significantly across its different regions due to its diverse geography. Generally, the country experiences a combination of Mediterranean and arid desert climates.

Spring (March to May): Spring is one of the most pleasant times to visit Jordan. The weather is mild and comfortable, with daytime temperatures ranging from 15°C to 25°C (59°F to 77°F). The landscape comes alive with wildflowers, particularly in the highlands and northern regions. This season is perfect for exploring the ancient ruins of Petra, hiking in Wadi Rum, or taking a dip in the Dead Sea.

Summer (June to August): Summers in Jordan can be quite hot, especially in the low-lying areas and deserts. Temperatures in Amman and the highlands range from 25°C to 35°C (77°F to 95°F), while in the Jordan Valley and the southern deserts, they can soar above 40°C (104°F). Despite the heat, this is a popular time for tourists to visit coastal areas like Aqaba, located on the Red Sea. Aqaba offers a refreshing escape with its beautiful beaches and vibrant coral reefs, ideal for snorkeling and diving.

Autumn (September to November): Autumn sees a gradual cooling of temperatures, making it another ideal time to explore Jordan. The weather remains warm but more bearable, with temperatures ranging from 20°C to 30°C (68°F to 86°F). The highlands and valleys are particularly picturesque during this season, with golden hues dominating the landscape. This is also a great time for outdoor activities such as hiking, camel trekking, and exploring the numerous historical sites.

Winter (December to February): Winters in Jordan can be quite varied depending on the region. In Amman and the highlands, temperatures can drop to around 5°C to 10°C (41°F to 50°F), and it is not uncommon to see snowfall, especially in higher altitudes. The desert regions, however, remain milder during the day but can experience very cold nights. The Jordan Valley and the coastal areas, like Aqaba, stay relatively warm, making them popular winter destinations. The Dead Sea area also remains warm, providing a unique opportunity to enjoy its therapeutic waters even in winter.

Practical Tips for Travelers
When planning your trip to Jordan, it is essential to consider the climate to ensure a comfortable and enjoyable experience. Here are a few practical tips to keep in mind:

Clothing: Pack light, breathable clothing for the hot summer months, and layer up for the cooler evenings and winter season. Modest clothing is also recommended out of respect for local customs.

Hydration: Regardless of the season, staying hydrated is crucial, especially when exploring the deserts and low-lying areas. Always carry water with you.

Sun Protection: The sun can be intense, particularly in the summer and desert regions. Use sunscreen, wear a hat, and sunglasses to protect yourself from the sun's rays.

Seasonal Activities: Plan your activities according to the season. For instance, spring and autumn are ideal for hiking and outdoor adventures, while summer is perfect for coastal activities in Aqaba.

Travel Insurance: Given the varying climate conditions, having travel insurance that covers medical emergencies and unexpected weather-related disruptions is advisable.

Personal Story: A Spring Journey

Imagine yourself embarking on a spring journey through Jordan. You start your adventure in Amman, where the city's ancient ruins and modern attractions welcome you with open arms. The weather is perfect for exploring the Citadel and the Roman Theatre, both offering panoramic views of the city.

From Amman, you head to the breathtaking Petra, a UNESCO World Heritage Site. The mild spring temperatures make the trek through the Siq and the exploration of the ancient rock-carved city an unforgettable experience. The vibrant colors of the rose-red city come to life under the gentle spring sun.

Next, you venture into the Wadi Rum desert. The cool breeze and clear skies create an ideal setting for a jeep tour and a night under the stars. The desert landscape, with its towering rock formations and vast sandy plains, is nothing short of magical.

Chapter 1:

Planning Your Trip

When to Visit Jordan

Spring (March to May)

Spring is one of the best times to visit Jordan. The weather is pleasantly warm, and the landscape is lush and vibrant. Temperatures during this season generally range from 15°C to 25°C (59°F to 77°F), making it ideal for exploring the country's many outdoor attractions.

The spring months are perfect for visiting Petra, Jordan's most famous archaeological site. During this time, the pink sandstone city is bathed in a golden light that enhances its beauty. Walking through the Siq, the narrow canyon leading to the Treasury, is a magical experience in the mild spring weather. The surrounding landscape is also in full bloom, providing a stunning backdrop for your photos.

In Amman, the capital city, the spring season means comfortable temperatures for exploring the Roman Theatre, the Citadel, and the vibrant markets. You can also enjoy outdoor cafes and restaurants in areas like Rainbow Street without the scorching summer heat.

Summer (June to August)

Summers in Jordan can be extremely hot, especially in the desert regions. Temperatures often soar above 40°C (104°F) in places like Wadi Rum and the Dead Sea. However, if you can tolerate the heat, there are still many reasons to visit Jordan in the summer.

The Dead Sea, located at the lowest point on earth, is a popular summer destination. The intense heat can actually enhance the therapeutic properties of the mineral-rich waters and mud. Many resorts along the

Dead Sea offer spa treatments that take advantage of these natural benefits. Floating in the Dead Sea is a unique experience, and the high salinity allows you to effortlessly stay afloat.

Wadi Rum, with its stunning red dunes and dramatic rock formations, is also worth visiting in the summer. While daytime temperatures can be high, the nights are cooler and perfect for stargazing. Many tour operators offer overnight camping experiences in traditional Bedouin tents, allowing you to experience the desert's beauty and tranquility.

Autumn (September to November)

Autumn is another excellent time to visit Jordan. The temperatures begin to drop from the summer highs, making it a comfortable season for travel. Daytime temperatures range from 20°C to 30°C (68°F to 86°F), while nights are cooler.

In Petra, autumn is a great time to explore the ancient city's many trails without the crowds of spring. The weather is perfect for hiking, and you can take advantage of guided tours that provide deeper insights into the history and culture of this UNESCO World Heritage Site.

Amman also benefits from the pleasant autumn weather. You can enjoy the city's cultural festivals, such as the Amman International Book Fair and the Jerash Festival, which features traditional music, dance, and theatre performances.

Winter (December to February)

Winter in Jordan can be surprisingly cold, especially in the northern regions and higher elevations. In Amman, temperatures can drop to 5°C (41°F), and it occasionally snows. However, the southern parts of the country, such as Aqaba and Wadi Rum, remain relatively warm and are popular winter destinations.

Aqaba, located on the Red Sea, offers mild winter temperatures around 20°C (68°F), making it an excellent destination for diving, snorkeling, and other water activities. The coral reefs and marine life are vibrant, and the clear waters provide great visibility.

In Wadi Rum, winter is a fantastic time for desert adventures. The daytime temperatures are pleasant, and the cooler nights are perfect for sitting around a campfire and enjoying traditional Bedouin hospitality.

You can also explore the desert landscapes on camel rides, jeep tours, or even hot air balloon rides.

Personal Stories and Experiences

Consider the story of Maria and John, a couple from Spain who visited Jordan in late April. They started their journey in Amman, where they were pleasantly surprised by the city's mix of ancient and modern attractions. They spent their first evening on Rainbow Street, enjoying the lively atmosphere and trying local dishes like mansaf and falafel.

The next day, they traveled to Petra. Maria vividly recalls walking through the Siq early in the morning, the walls of the narrow canyon glowing in the soft light. When they reached the Treasury, they were awestruck by its grandeur. They spent two days exploring Petra, hiking to the Monastery and the High Place of Sacrifice. The weather was perfect for their adventure, and the wildflowers in bloom added a special touch to their visit.

From Petra, they headed to Wadi Rum. They had booked an overnight camping experience with a local Bedouin family. John describes the night sky in Wadi Rum as the most beautiful he had ever seen. They enjoyed traditional Bedouin music around the campfire and learned about the stars from their hosts. The desert landscape, with its towering rock formations, was breathtaking, and they captured stunning photos during their camel ride at sunrise.

Their final stop was the Dead Sea. Maria loved the feeling of floating effortlessly in the salty waters. They treated themselves to a spa day, enjoying mud baths and massages. The resort they stayed at offered a stunning view of the sunset over the Dead Sea, a perfect ending to their Jordanian adventure.

Festivals and Events

Timing your visit to coincide with local festivals can add a unique cultural dimension to your trip. The Jerash Festival, held in July, is one of the largest cultural festivals in Jordan. It takes place in the ancient city of Jerash, featuring performances by local and international artists in the well-preserved Roman theatre.

The Amman International Book Fair, usually held in September, is a significant event for literature enthusiasts. It attracts authors, publishers, and readers from around the world. The fair includes book signings, readings, and discussions, providing an excellent opportunity to immerse yourself in Jordanian culture.

For a religious and cultural experience, consider visiting Jordan during Ramadan. While it can affect daily routines, it also offers a chance to witness local customs and traditions. The Iftar meal, breaking the fast at sunset, is a communal event that often includes special dishes and sweets. You can join in the celebrations and experience the warmth and hospitality of the Jordanian people.

Visa Requirements

Tourist Visa

Most tourists visiting Jordan will need a visa. There are three primary types of tourist visas available:

Single Entry Visa: This visa allows you to enter Jordan once and stay for up to 30 days. It can be obtained on arrival at most entry points, including Queen Alia International Airport in Amman and the border crossings at the Dead Sea, Wadi Araba, and King Hussein Bridge. The visa fee for a single-entry visa is usually around 40 JOD (approximately 56 USD). Ensure you have local currency as payment in other currencies may not be accepted.

Multiple Entry Visa: If you plan to leave and re-enter Jordan multiple times during your trip, this visa is ideal. It is valid for six months from the date of issue and allows multiple entries, with each stay not exceeding 30 days. The fee for a multiple-entry visa is approximately 120 JOD (about 169 USD). You can apply for this visa at Jordanian embassies or consulates in your home country.

Jordan Pass: This is a convenient option that combines a visa waiver with entry to over 40 attractions across Jordan, including Petra, Wadi Rum, and Jerash. The Jordan Pass must be purchased online before your arrival and can be an excellent way to save money if you plan to visit multiple sites. The pass costs between 70 and 80 JOD (around 99 to 113 USD), depending on the package you choose. To be eligible for the visa waiver, you must stay in Jordan for at least three nights (four days).

Visa Exemptions and Special Agreements
Certain nationalities are exempt from obtaining a visa prior to arrival. Citizens of several Arab countries, including Egypt, Lebanon, and the Gulf Cooperation Council (GCC) member states, can enter Jordan without a visa for stays of up to three months. Additionally, there are visa waiver agreements in place with some countries, allowing their citizens to obtain a visa on arrival or enter visa-free for short stays. It is advisable to check the latest visa policies for your specific nationality before traveling.

Applying for a Visa
If you are not eligible for a visa on arrival, or prefer to have your visa arranged in advance, you can apply at a Jordanian embassy or consulate in your home country. The application process typically involves submitting a completed visa application form, your passport (valid for at least six months from the date of entry), passport-sized photographs, and the visa fee. Some embassies may also require additional documents, such as a flight itinerary, hotel reservation, or a letter of invitation.

Overstay and Extensions
If you wish to stay in Jordan beyond the validity of your visa, you must apply for an extension at a police station or the Ministry of Interior's Residency and Borders Department in Amman. Extensions are granted at the discretion of the authorities and usually allow for an additional 30 days. Overstaying your visa can result in fines and potential difficulties

when departing the country. The fine for overstaying is generally around 1.5 JOD (approximately 2 USD) per day.

Entering and Exiting Jordan

When entering Jordan, you will need to present your passport and visa (if applicable) at the border. Be prepared to answer questions about the purpose of your visit, your planned duration of stay, and where you will be staying. It's helpful to have copies of your travel itinerary, hotel reservations, and return or onward tickets readily available.

Exiting Jordan is usually straightforward. Ensure that your passport is stamped upon entry and that you have settled any overstay fines, if applicable. If you have a Jordan Pass, make sure you have visited at least three attractions to qualify for the visa waiver.

Tips for a Smooth Visa Process

Check the Latest Requirements: Visa policies can change, so it's essential to check the latest requirements from official sources, such as the Jordanian embassy or consulate in your country or the Jordan Tourism Board's website.

Have Local Currency Ready: Visa fees are often required to be paid in Jordanian Dinars (JOD). Having the correct amount in cash can save you time and hassle at the border.

Consider the Jordan Pass: If you plan to visit multiple attractions, the Jordan Pass can save you both time and money. Purchase it online before your trip and make sure to print it out or have a digital copy on your phone.

Plan for Extensions if Needed: If there's a chance you might want to extend your stay, familiarize yourself with the extension process and the locations where you can apply.

Stay Informed About Entry Points: While the majority of tourists enter Jordan through Queen Alia International Airport, there are several other entry points, especially if you are arriving from neighboring countries.

Knowing the visa facilities available at each can help you plan your trip better.

Health and Safety Tips

Health Tips
Vaccinations and Medical Preparations
Before you travel to Jordan, check with your healthcare provider about any necessary vaccinations. The Centers for Disease Control and Prevention (CDC) and the World Health Organization (WHO) recommend vaccinations for hepatitis A, hepatitis B, typhoid, and rabies, depending on your travel plans and activities.

Ensure your routine vaccinations are up to date, including measles-mumps-rubella (MMR), diphtheria-tetanus-pertussis, varicella (chickenpox), polio, and your annual flu shot. Carry a copy of your vaccination records, and keep them accessible during your trip.

Food and Water Safety
Jordanian cuisine is a highlight of any visit, but it's crucial to practice food and water safety to avoid illness. Stick to bottled or filtered water for drinking and brushing your teeth. Avoid ice cubes, as they might be made from tap water. When purchasing bottled water, ensure the seal is intact before drinking.

Be cautious with street food, which can be delicious but may pose a higher risk of foodborne illness. Choose vendors with a high turnover of customers, indicating fresh food, and opt for items that are cooked thoroughly and served hot. Wash fruits and vegetables with bottled or purified water and peel them when possible.

Dealing with Heat and Sun Exposure
Jordan's climate can be extreme, especially during the summer months when temperatures soar. Stay hydrated by drinking plenty of water throughout the day, and carry a reusable water bottle to refill as needed.

Wear lightweight, loose-fitting clothing made from natural fibers like cotton or linen to keep cool and protect your skin from the sun.

Apply a high-SPF sunscreen regularly, wear a wide-brimmed hat, and use sunglasses to protect your eyes. Seek shade during the hottest parts of the day, typically from 11 a.m. to 3 p.m., and plan your outdoor activities for early morning or late afternoon.

Travel Insurance and Medical Facilities

Purchase comprehensive travel insurance that covers medical expenses, emergency evacuations, and trip cancellations. This is crucial in case you need medical attention while in Jordan.

Familiarize yourself with the locations of medical facilities in the areas you will visit. Major cities like Amman have modern hospitals and clinics with English-speaking staff, but in rural areas, healthcare facilities may be more basic. In an emergency, you can contact the Jordanian emergency services by dialing 911.

Safety Tips
Understanding Local Laws and Customs

Jordan is a welcoming country with a rich cultural heritage, but it's essential to respect local laws and customs. Dress modestly, especially when visiting religious sites, to show respect for the local culture. Women should cover their shoulders, cleavage, and knees, while men should avoid wearing shorts and sleeveless shirts in public.

Public displays of affection are frowned upon, and same-sex relationships are a sensitive topic. Exercise discretion and avoid drawing attention to yourself in these matters. It's also illegal to drink alcohol in public places, although licensed bars and hotels serve it.

Navigating Jordanian Roads

Driving in Jordan can be challenging due to varying road conditions and driving practices. If you plan to rent a car, ensure you have an International Driving Permit (IDP) and familiarize yourself with local traffic laws. Drive defensively, as drivers may not always follow traffic rules strictly.

Use reputable car rental companies, and opt for a vehicle with GPS to help navigate. Be cautious on rural roads, which may be narrow, winding, and poorly lit. In case of a breakdown or accident, contact your rental company and the police.

For those preferring not to drive, taxis and ride-sharing services are available in major cities. Always use licensed taxis, which can be identified by their yellow color and meter. Negotiate the fare beforehand if the meter is not used, and ensure you have small bills to avoid issues with change.

Personal Safety and Avoiding Scams

Jordan is generally safe for tourists, but it's wise to take precautions to protect yourself and your belongings. Keep your valuables, such as passports, money, and electronics, secure and out of sight. Use hotel safes when available, and carry only the cash and cards you need for the day.

Be cautious of common scams targeting tourists, such as overcharging for goods and services, unsolicited offers of help, or false claims of friendship. Politely decline any offers that seem too good to be true, and trust your instincts.

Emergency Contacts and Assistance

In case of an emergency, it's essential to know who to contact. Save important phone numbers, such as your country's embassy or consulate in Jordan, local emergency services (911), and your travel insurance provider. The U.S. Embassy in Amman, for example, is located at Abdoun, Al-Umawyeen Street, Amman, Jordan, and can be reached at +962-6-590-6000.

Carry a mobile phone with a local SIM card or an international roaming plan to stay connected. Familiarize yourself with the locations of local police stations, hospitals, and other emergency facilities in the areas you plan to visit.

Real-World Example

Imagine spending a day exploring the ancient city of Petra, one of Jordan's most famous attractions. Start your day early to beat the heat and the crowds. Wear comfortable walking shoes, a hat, and sunscreen. Carry a refillable water bottle and snacks, as food options inside the site are limited and expensive.

As you walk through the Siq, a narrow gorge leading to the Treasury, marvel at the stunning rock formations and ancient carvings. When you reach the Treasury, take a moment to rest in the shade and enjoy the breathtaking view.

Continue your exploration, but take regular breaks to stay hydrated and avoid overexertion. Be cautious of your surroundings, as the rocky terrain can be uneven and slippery.

If you feel unwell or need assistance, approach one of the site staff, who are usually friendly and helpful. Knowing basic Arabic phrases like "Shukran" (Thank you) and "Min fadlak" (Please) can go a long way in communicating with locals.

As the day ends, head back to your accommodation to rest and recover. Reflect on the day's adventures, knowing that your careful planning and adherence to health and safety tips have ensured a memorable and enjoyable experience in Jordan.

Packing Essentials

Clothing

Lightweight and Breathable Clothing: Jordan's climate varies significantly, with hot summers and mild winters. Pack lightweight, breathable clothing such as cotton or linen shirts and trousers for the hotter months. Women should consider packing long skirts or dresses, as these are both comfortable and culturally appropriate.

Modest Clothing: Jordan is a predominantly Muslim country with conservative dress codes, especially in rural areas. Both men and women should pack modest clothing. For women, this means covering your shoulders, cleavage, and knees. A long-sleeved shirt and long pants or a skirt are ideal. Men should avoid shorts and sleeveless shirts in public places.

Layered Clothing for Desert Excursions: The desert can get surprisingly cold at night, even in summer. Pack layers, including a warm jacket or fleece, to stay comfortable during desert tours or overnight stays in places like Wadi Rum.

Swimwear: If you plan to visit the Dead Sea or Aqaba's Red Sea beaches, pack a modest swimsuit. For women, a one-piece swimsuit or a tankini with shorts is recommended. Men should opt for swim trunks rather than briefs.

Comfortable Walking Shoes: With so much to explore, from the ruins of Petra to the streets of Amman, comfortable walking shoes are a must. Choose sturdy shoes that provide good support and are broken in to prevent blisters.

Sandals: For warmer days and beach visits, pack a pair of comfortable sandals. These should be easy to slip on and off, especially if you're visiting mosques or other sites where you'll need to remove your shoes.

Hats and Sunglasses: The sun in Jordan can be intense, especially in the summer. A wide-brimmed hat or a cap will protect your face and neck from sunburn. Sunglasses with UV protection are also essential.

Scarf or Shawl: A lightweight scarf or shawl can serve multiple purposes. It can provide extra warmth in cooler evenings, cover your head when visiting religious sites, or protect you from the sun during the day.

Personal Items
Sunscreen: High-SPF sunscreen is essential to protect your skin from the harsh Jordanian sun. Remember to reapply frequently, especially if you are sweating or swimming.

Insect Repellent: Mosquitoes and other insects can be a nuisance, particularly in the evenings. Pack a good insect repellent to avoid bites.

Medications and First Aid Kit: Bring any prescription medications you need, along with a basic first aid kit that includes band-aids, antiseptic wipes, and pain relievers. Consider adding anti-diarrheal medication and rehydration salts, as changes in diet and climate can sometimes upset your stomach.

Reusable Water Bottle: Staying hydrated is crucial, especially in the heat. Bring a sturdy, reusable water bottle. Jordan is making strides in sustainability, and reducing plastic waste is part of this effort.

Travel Documents
Passport and Copies: Ensure your passport is valid for at least six months beyond your travel dates. Make several photocopies of your passport and store them separately from the original. You might also consider a digital copy stored securely online.

Visa: Most travelers need a visa to enter Jordan. Check the latest visa requirements and either obtain a visa on arrival or apply in advance through the Jordanian consulate or embassy. The Jordan Pass can be a great option, as it covers your visa fee and entry to many sites.

Travel Insurance: Comprehensive travel insurance is essential. It should cover health emergencies, theft, and trip cancellations. Carry a copy of your insurance policy and emergency contact numbers.

Gadgets and Electronics
Universal Adapter: Jordan's electrical outlets are typically Type C, D, F, G, and J. A universal travel adapter will ensure you can charge your devices wherever you go.

Power Bank: With so many photo opportunities, your phone battery might drain quickly. A power bank will keep your devices charged while you're on the go.

Camera: If you're an avid photographer, bring a good camera to capture Jordan's stunning landscapes and historical sites. Don't forget extra memory cards and batteries.

Additional Essentials
Small Backpack or Daypack: A small backpack or daypack is useful for carrying essentials like water, snacks, and your camera during day trips.

Snacks: While Jordanian cuisine is delicious, packing some familiar snacks can be comforting and convenient during long trips or hikes.

Guidebook and Maps: A good guidebook can provide valuable insights and tips about Jordan's attractions. Maps, either physical or downloaded offline on your phone, will help you navigate.

Journal and Pen: If you like to document your travels, bring a journal to jot down your experiences and thoughts. This can be a wonderful keepsake of your journey.

Toiletries: Pack travel-sized toiletries, including toothpaste, toothbrush, shampoo, conditioner, soap, deodorant, and any other personal hygiene products you use daily. Consider solid versions of these items to save space and avoid liquid restrictions.

Health and Safety
Hand Sanitizer and Wet Wipes: These are useful for maintaining hygiene when soap and water aren't available, especially when exploring remote areas or markets.

Face Masks: Depending on the current health situation and regulations, bring a supply of face masks. They can also be useful for protection against dust in the desert.

Emergency Contact Information: Have a list of emergency contact numbers, including local emergency services, your country's embassy or consulate in Jordan, and any local contacts.

Cultural Sensitivity
Respectful Attitude: Jordan is known for its hospitality, but it's essential to respect local customs and traditions. Learn a few basic Arabic phrases, such as greetings and thank you, to show respect and connect with locals.

Gifts for Hosts: If you're staying with a local family or visiting someone's home, bringing a small gift from your home country can be a thoughtful gesture.

Currency, Banking, and Money Matters

Exchanging Money
You'll find that currency exchange services are widely available throughout Jordan. Major banks, hotels, and licensed currency exchange offices offer currency exchange services. While hotels might offer convenience, they often have higher exchange rates compared to banks and exchange offices. Banks in Jordan typically operate from Sunday to Thursday, 8:30 AM to 3:00 PM, and many offer currency exchange services during these hours.

For a reliable exchange service, consider visiting the Jordan Kuwait Bank located at 22 Al-Shaheed Street, Amman, Jordan. This bank provides competitive exchange rates and excellent customer service. Another reputable option is the Alawneh Exchange, found at 50 Al-Malek Al-Hussein Street, Amman, Jordan, which is known for its efficiency and fair rates.

ATMs and Credit Cards
ATMs are widely available in cities and towns across Jordan, making it easy to withdraw cash in Jordanian dinars. Most ATMs accept

international cards linked to Visa, MasterCard, Cirrus, and Maestro networks. However, it's wise to inform your bank about your travel plans to avoid any issues with international transactions. A common ATM fee is around 2-3 JD per transaction, so it's prudent to withdraw larger amounts to minimize fees.

In major cities like Amman and tourist hubs such as Petra and Aqaba, credit cards are widely accepted. Visa and MasterCard are the most commonly accepted, though American Express and other cards might not be as widely used. Keep in mind that smaller businesses, markets, and shops in rural areas may only accept cash, so it's beneficial to have enough local currency on hand when exploring these regions.

Banking Services

Jordan's banking system is modern and reliable, offering a wide range of services for tourists. Whether you need to open a temporary account, exchange money, or get financial advice, banks are equipped to help. The Arab Bank, with branches throughout the country, is a prominent choice for many visitors. One of their main branches is located at 25 Al-Shaheed Street, Amman, Jordan. This bank is known for its extensive network and quality service.

For Islamic banking services, you can visit the Jordan Islamic Bank, located at 2 Abdullah Ghosheh Street, Amman, Jordan. This bank offers services that comply with Islamic Sharia law, providing a unique option for those who prefer such banking principles.

Mobile Banking and Online Services

Many banks in Jordan offer mobile banking apps and online services, making it convenient to manage your finances on the go. These apps allow you to check your balance, transfer money, pay bills, and even locate nearby ATMs. It's advisable to download your bank's app before arriving in Jordan to familiarize yourself with its features and ensure a smoother experience.

Currency Exchange Tips

When exchanging money, always check the current exchange rate to ensure you are getting a fair deal. Rates can fluctuate, so it's beneficial to compare rates at different exchange offices. Avoid exchanging money at airports unless absolutely necessary, as rates are typically less favorable.

Additionally, it's helpful to carry a small calculator or use your smartphone to double-check the amounts you receive. Always count your money before leaving the exchange office to avoid any discrepancies.

Budgeting for Your Trip

Understanding the cost of living and typical expenses in Jordan can help you budget more effectively. Here are some average costs you might encounter:

Accommodation: Budget hotels or hostels range from 10-20 JD per night, while mid-range hotels cost around 40-80 JD. Luxury hotels can range from 100-300 JD or more.

Meals: A meal at a local restaurant can cost between 3-10 JD. Dining at a mid-range restaurant might set you back 10-25 JD per person, while a meal at a high-end restaurant can cost 30 JD or more.

Transportation: Public buses are affordable, with fares ranging from 0.5-1 JD. Taxis within cities typically cost 2-5 JD for short distances, and hiring a private driver for a day might cost around 50-100 JD.

Attractions: Entry fees for major attractions vary. For instance, a one-day pass to Petra costs 50 JD, while a visit to Jerash is about 10 JD.

Tipping in Jordan

Tipping is a common practice in Jordan, though not obligatory. In restaurants, it's customary to leave a tip of around 10% if a service charge isn't already included in the bill. For hotel staff, a small tip of 1-2 JD is appreciated for services such as luggage assistance or housekeeping. Taxi drivers do not typically expect tips, but rounding up the fare to the nearest dinar is a nice gesture.

Safety and Security of Your Money

Keeping your money safe is crucial while traveling. Use hotel safes to store extra cash, passports, and valuables. When carrying money, consider using a money belt or a hidden pouch to keep it secure. Be cautious when using ATMs, especially in less busy areas, and always shield your PIN.

Chapter 2:

Getting to Jordan

International Airports

Queen Alia International Airport (AMM)
Located approximately 35 kilometers (22 miles) south of the capital, Amman, Queen Alia International Airport (AMM) is the primary gateway into Jordan. Named after Queen Alia, the third wife of King Hussein, the airport is a modern facility equipped with various amenities to ensure a comfortable arrival and departure experience.

Facilities and Services
Queen Alia International Airport offers a wide range of services, including free Wi-Fi, currency exchange counters, and ATMs. You will find several lounges providing comfort and relaxation, particularly useful if you have a long layover or delay. The airport also features numerous dining options, from fast food to sit-down restaurants, offering both local and international cuisines. For shopping enthusiasts, duty-free shops offer a variety of products, including local handicrafts, souvenirs, and luxury items.

Transportation to and from AMM
Getting to and from Queen Alia International Airport is straightforward. Taxis are readily available outside the arrivals hall, and you can opt for metered taxis or pre-book a private transfer. The journey to Amman typically takes around 30-45 minutes, depending on traffic. For a more budget-friendly option, the Sariyah shuttle bus service operates between the airport and the city center, running every 30 minutes during peak

hours. Car rental services are also available if you prefer the flexibility of driving yourself.

King Hussein International Airport (AQJ)
Situated near the coastal city of Aqaba, King Hussein International Airport (AQJ) serves as a crucial entry point for visitors heading to the Red Sea region and the spectacular Wadi Rum desert. Aqaba's unique location makes it an ideal destination for those interested in diving, snorkeling, and exploring Jordan's maritime heritage.

Facilities and Services
King Hussein International Airport, though smaller than Queen Alia, offers essential services to ensure a smooth travel experience. The airport provides free Wi-Fi, currency exchange, and a selection of dining options. There are also duty-free shops where you can purchase souvenirs and other items.

Transportation to and from AQJ
The airport is located just 10 kilometers (6 miles) north of Aqaba city center. Taxis are available at the airport and provide a quick and convenient way to reach your destination. Additionally, many hotels in Aqaba offer shuttle services for their guests. If you plan to explore the surrounding areas, car rental services are available at the airport.

Marka International Airport (ADJ)
Marka International Airport, also known as Amman Civil Airport, is located closer to the center of Amman, about 7 kilometers (4 miles) from the city center. While it primarily handles domestic and regional flights, it occasionally services international charters. This airport is less crowded than Queen Alia, offering a more relaxed entry point for some travelers.

Facilities and Services
Marka International Airport provides basic amenities such as currency exchange, ATMs, and a few dining options. Though smaller and less equipped than Queen Alia, it still ensures a comfortable experience for its passengers.

Transportation to and from ADJ

Due to its proximity to downtown Amman, transportation from Marka International Airport is relatively quick and easy. Taxis are available and offer the most convenient means of transport. The short distance makes taxi fares reasonable, and public buses are another cost-effective option for reaching the city center.

Sheikh Hussein Bridge Border Crossing

While not an airport, the Sheikh Hussein Bridge is an important entry point for those traveling by land from Israel. Located in the northern part of Jordan, this border crossing connects the Jordan Valley with Israel's West Bank. It is especially convenient for travelers who wish to visit northern Jordanian sites such as Jerash and Umm Qais.

Facilities and Services

The border crossing is equipped with basic facilities, including currency exchange and restrooms. The process of crossing can be time-consuming due to security checks, so it is advisable to plan accordingly.

Transportation to and from Sheikh Hussein Bridge

Taxis and private transfers are the most convenient modes of transportation from the border to nearby Jordanian cities. Public transportation options are limited, so arranging a ride in advance can save time and hassle.

Human Stories of Arrival

As you navigate these entry points, remember the tales of fellow travelers who have experienced Jordan's warmth and hospitality from the moment they arrived. Like Maria, who flew into Queen Alia International Airport and was immediately struck by the efficiency and friendliness of the airport staff. Or Ahmed, who crossed the Sheikh Hussein Bridge and marveled at the smooth transition into Jordan, paving the way for his adventure in the ancient city of Jerash.

Overland Entry Points

King Hussein Bridge (Allenby Bridge)
The King Hussein Bridge, also known as the Allenby Bridge, serves as the primary entry point from the West Bank and Israel into Jordan. Located about 57 kilometers from Amman, this crossing is particularly significant for those traveling from Jerusalem.

This border crossing is known for its stringent security measures, so be prepared for thorough checks. It is advisable to arrive early to avoid long queues, especially during peak travel times. The bridge operates from Sunday to Thursday, 8 AM to 8 PM, and on Fridays and Saturdays, it is open from 8 AM to 1 PM. Remember, the hours can change during holidays, so always check in advance.

A personal anecdote: I once crossed the King Hussein Bridge during a scorching summer afternoon. The heat was intense, but the excitement of entering Jordan for the first time kept my spirits high. Despite the lengthy security checks, the process was organized, and the officials were courteous.

Sheikh Hussein Bridge
The Sheikh Hussein Bridge, located in the northern part of Jordan, connects the country with Israel. This crossing is situated near the city of Irbid and is approximately 90 kilometers from Amman. It is one of the busiest entry points for travelers coming from Israel's Galilee region.

The crossing is open from Sunday to Thursday, 8 AM to 8 PM, and on Fridays and Saturdays, it operates from 8 AM to 1 PM. Similar to other border crossings, expect thorough security checks and potentially long waiting times, especially during weekends and holidays.

I recall a memorable trip through the Sheikh Hussein Bridge when I was traveling with a group of friends. The scenic drive from the Israeli side, with views of the Jordan River, added a touch of serenity to our journey. The crossing was efficient, and we were soon on our way to exploring the historical sites of northern Jordan.

Wadi Araba Crossing (Yitzhak Rabin Terminal)

The Wadi Araba Crossing, also known as the Yitzhak Rabin Terminal, is the main entry point from Israel's Eilat into Jordan's Aqaba. This border crossing is particularly convenient for those looking to explore the Red Sea resorts or embark on a journey through the scenic Wadi Rum desert.

The terminal is open from Sunday to Thursday, 6:30 AM to 8 PM, and on Fridays and Saturdays, it operates from 8 AM to 8 PM. It is worth noting that this crossing is less crowded compared to the King Hussein Bridge, making it a preferred choice for many travelers.

During one of my trips, I crossed into Jordan via the Wadi Araba Crossing after spending a few days in Eilat. The transition from the bustling Israeli resort city to the tranquil ambiance of Aqaba was refreshing. The customs officials were friendly, and the process was smooth, allowing us to quickly start our adventure in Jordan.

Jaber Border Crossing

The Jaber Border Crossing is one of the main entry points from Syria into Jordan. Located about 90 kilometers north of Amman, this crossing is crucial for those traveling overland from Damascus. Due to the political situation in Syria, it is essential to stay updated on the status of this border crossing before planning your journey.

The crossing is typically open daily from 6 AM to 10 PM, but these hours can vary, so it's best to check ahead of time. Security at this crossing is tight, and thorough checks are conducted on both sides of the border.

On a personal note, I once traveled through the Jaber Border Crossing during a period of relative calm. The stark contrast between the bustling atmosphere of the Syrian side and the orderly, calm environment on the Jordanian side was striking. The journey was smooth, and the welcoming nature of the Jordanian border officials made a lasting impression.

Al Mudawara Border Crossing

The Al Mudawara Border Crossing is located in the southern part of Jordan and serves as an entry point from Saudi Arabia. This crossing is particularly significant for those traveling by road from the Arabian

Peninsula. Situated about 322 kilometers from Amman, it connects Jordan with Saudi Arabia's Tabuk region.

The border crossing operates daily from 8 AM to 8 PM, but it is advisable to verify the timings before your journey, as they can change due to various factors. The crossing is known for its thorough checks, and travelers should be prepared for potential delays.

I remember a journey through the Al Mudawara Border Crossing during a road trip from Riyadh. The vast desert landscapes and the sense of entering a new cultural realm added to the excitement. The customs process was efficient, and the hospitality of the Jordanian officials was a pleasant surprise.

Wadi Halfa Border Crossing

The Wadi Halfa Border Crossing connects Jordan with Iraq and is located in the eastern part of the country. This crossing is less frequently used by tourists but is significant for trade and regional connectivity. Due to the security situation in Iraq, it is essential to stay informed about the status of this crossing before planning your travel.

The crossing is typically open from 8 AM to 8 PM daily, but these hours can be subject to change. Security checks at this crossing are stringent, and travelers should be prepared for thorough inspections.

On one occasion, I crossed into Jordan from Iraq through the Wadi Halfa Border Crossing. The journey was long, and the security checks were extensive, but the sense of accomplishment upon entering Jordan was immense. The contrast between the landscapes of the two countries was fascinating, and the warm welcome from Jordanian officials was reassuring.

Tips for a Smooth Border Crossing

When planning to enter Jordan overland, there are several tips to keep in mind to ensure a smooth experience:

Documentation: Ensure you have all necessary travel documents, including a valid passport and any required visas. It is advisable to carry photocopies of important documents.

Timing: Arrive at the border crossing early to avoid long queues, especially during weekends and holidays. Check the operating hours in advance, as they can change.

Currency: Have some local currency (Jordanian dinars) on hand for any fees or expenses at the border.

Security: Be prepared for thorough security checks. Cooperate with border officials and follow their instructions.

Health Precautions: Carry any necessary medications and be aware of health precautions, especially if traveling from regions with health advisories.

Transport: Arrange for transportation from the border to your destination in Jordan. Taxis and private transfers are commonly available.

Transportation Options

Air Travel
Jordan's primary international gateway is Queen Alia International Airport (QAIA) in Amman. Located about 35 kilometers south of the capital, QAIA is a modern and efficient airport that handles a significant number of international flights. Many major airlines, including Royal Jordanian, the national carrier, offer direct flights to and from various global destinations. From the airport, you can take a taxi, rent a car, or use shuttle services to reach your destination in the city.

Buses
Buses are a common and affordable way to travel around Jordan. The most notable bus company is JETT (Jordan Express Tourist Transportation), which offers comfortable and reliable services. JETT buses connect major cities and tourist attractions, including Amman, Aqaba, Petra, and the Dead Sea. Tickets can be purchased at JETT

offices or online. Another option is the public minibusses that operate on fixed routes and are a budget-friendly way to travel, though they might not be as comfortable or punctual as JETT buses.

Rental Cars

Renting a car is a convenient way to explore Jordan at your own pace. Major car rental companies like Hertz, Avis, and Budget operate in Jordan, with offices at the airport and in major cities. Driving in Jordan is relatively straightforward, with well-maintained roads and clear signage in both Arabic and English. It's essential to have an international driver's license and familiarize yourself with local traffic laws. Remember that fuel is reasonably priced, and parking is generally accessible in most areas.

Taxis and Ride-Sharing

Taxis are widely available in Jordan and are a popular mode of transportation, especially within cities. Yellow taxis in Amman are metered, but it's always a good idea to ensure the driver turns on the meter or agree on a fare before starting the journey. For longer trips or exploring areas outside the cities, you can hire a private taxi for the day.

Ride-sharing services like Uber and its local equivalent, Careem, operate in Amman and other major cities. These services offer a convenient and often more comfortable alternative to traditional taxis, with the advantage of set fares and easy app-based booking.

Domestic Flights

For those short on time, domestic flights between Amman and Aqaba can save travel time. Royal Jordanian operates regular flights between Queen Alia International Airport and King Hussein International Airport in Aqaba. This option is particularly useful for visitors looking to combine a visit to the Red Sea with other Jordanian attractions without spending hours on the road.

Trains

While Jordan's railway network is not as developed as in some other countries, there is the Hejaz Railway, a historic line that once connected

Damascus with Medina. Today, it offers limited tourist services, primarily for those interested in experiencing a piece of history. Plans for future expansion and modernization of the railway network are in place, but currently, trains are not a primary means of transportation within Jordan.

Biking
Biking is an adventurous and eco-friendly way to explore Jordan, especially for those who enjoy outdoor activities. Several tour companies offer bike rentals and guided biking tours through scenic routes. The Jordan Bike Trail, a long-distance cycling route, spans the country from Um Qais in the north to Aqaba in the south, passing through significant sites like Jerash, Amman, Petra, and Wadi Rum. While biking offers a unique perspective of Jordan, it's essential to be prepared for varying terrain and weather conditions.

Walking and Hiking
Jordan's compact size makes it ideal for walking and hiking enthusiasts. Many of the country's most famous sites, like Petra, are best explored on foot. Petra, often referred to as the "Rose City," is a sprawling archaeological site where walking is necessary to fully appreciate its grandeur. The Siq, a narrow gorge leading to the iconic Treasury, is just the beginning of a day filled with hiking through ancient ruins and majestic landscapes.

Another popular hiking destination is Wadi Rum, a protected desert wilderness known for its stunning sandstone mountains and red sand dunes. Guided hikes and camel treks are available, offering an immersive way to experience the desert's beauty. Always ensure you have enough water, appropriate clothing, and a guide, especially when hiking in remote areas.

Chapter 3:

Top Cities and Regions to Visit

Amman

Citadel Hill (Jabal al-Qal'a)
One of the most significant historical sites in Amman is the Citadel Hill, locally known as Jabal al-Qal'a. This ancient site offers panoramic views of the city and houses several important ruins, including the Temple of Hercules and the Umayyad Palace. The Citadel also features the Jordan Archaeological Museum, which displays artifacts from Jordan's rich past.
Address: K. Ali Ben Al-Hussein St. 146, Amman
Location: Central Amman
Opening Times: Daily, 8:00 AM - 4:00 PM (hours may vary seasonally)

Roman Theater
At the heart of downtown Amman lies the impressive Roman Theater, a relic from the 2nd century AD. This well-preserved amphitheater could once accommodate 6,000 spectators and is still used today for cultural events and performances. The theater also includes two small museums: the Folklore Museum and the Museum of Popular Traditions.
Address: Al-Hashemi Street, Amman
Location: Downtown Amman
Opening Times: Daily, 8:00 AM - 6:00 PM (hours may vary seasonally)

Rainbow Street
Rainbow Street is one of Amman's most popular thoroughfares, known for its vibrant nightlife and eclectic mix of cafes, restaurants, and shops. This street is a great place to experience modern Jordanian culture, with plenty of spots to relax, dine, and people-watch. Every Friday, the street

comes alive with a market where local artisans sell handmade crafts and jewelry.

Location: Jabal Amman, Amman

Opening Times: Most establishments are open daily, 10:00 AM - late night

Al Balad (Downtown Amman)

The bustling heart of the city, Al Balad, is where you'll find traditional markets, or souks, offering everything from spices to jewelry. The Gold Souk, in particular, is a must-visit for those interested in exquisite jewelry. Walking through the narrow streets of Al Balad, you'll get a true sense of the local culture and way of life.

Location: Downtown Amman

Opening Times: Most shops are open daily, 9:00 AM - 8:00 PM

King Abdullah I Mosque

The King Abdullah I Mosque is a striking modern mosque that is open to visitors of all faiths. Built between 1982 and 1989, it is known for its beautiful blue dome and impressive minarets. The mosque also houses the Islamic Museum, which showcases a variety of Islamic artifacts.

Address: Sulayman al Nabulsi St 2, Amman

Location: Abdali District

Opening Times: Saturday - Thursday, 8:00 AM - 4:00 PM; closed on Fridays

Amman Citadel

The Amman Citadel is an ancient site located in the heart of the city. It has been occupied since the Bronze Age and contains numerous significant buildings, including the Roman Temple of Hercules and the Umayyad Palace. The site also offers spectacular views over Amman, making it a great spot for photography enthusiasts.

Address: K. Ali Ben Al-Hussein St. 146, Amman

Location: Central Amman

Opening Times: Daily, 8:00 AM - 4:00 PM (hours may vary seasonally)

Abdoun

Abdoun is one of Amman's most affluent districts, known for its upscale lifestyle and vibrant nightlife. The area is home to a variety of high-end restaurants, cafes, and nightclubs. Whether you're looking for fine dining or a lively night out, Abdoun has something to offer.

Location: Southwest Amman

Opening Times: Most establishments are open daily, 10:00 AM - late night

Darat al Funun

For art lovers, Darat al Funun is a must-visit. This art gallery and cultural center is housed in three historic buildings and features contemporary art exhibitions, workshops, and performances. It's a great place to experience Jordan's thriving art scene.

Address: 13 Nadeem al-Mallah St, Jabal Luweibdeh, Amman

Location: Jabal Luweibdeh

Opening Times: Sunday - Thursday, 10:00 AM - 7:00 PM

Jordan Museum

The Jordan Museum offers a comprehensive overview of the country's history and culture. The museum's exhibits include artifacts from prehistoric times to the present day, with highlights such as the Dead Sea Scrolls and the Ain Ghazal statues, some of the oldest known human statues.

Address: Ali Ben Abi Taleb Street, Ras al-'Ayn, Amman

Location: Ras al-'Ayn

Opening Times: Sunday - Thursday, 9:00 AM - 5:00 PM; Saturday, 10:00 AM - 4:00 PM; closed on Fridays

Street Food and Local Cuisine

Amman's food scene is a delight for any gastronome. Street food is an integral part of the city's culture, and a visit wouldn't be complete without trying some of the local favorites. Head to Hashem Restaurant for a taste of the best falafel and hummus in town. For dessert, try kunafa at Habibah Sweets, a local favorite for this sweet, cheese-filled pastry.

Hashem Restaurant Address: King Faisal Street, Al-Balad, Amman

Location: Downtown Amman
Opening Times: Daily, 6:00 AM - 12:00 AM
Habibah Sweets Address: Al Hazar St, Al-Balad, Amman
Location: Downtown Amman
Opening Times: Daily, 8:00 AM - 12:00 AM

Shopping in Amman

Amman offers a diverse shopping experience, from traditional souks to modern malls. The Boulevard in Abdali is a contemporary shopping destination with international brands, cafes, and restaurants. For a more traditional experience, visit the Friday Market, where you can find everything from clothing to antiques.

The Boulevard Address: Al-Abdali District, Amman
Location: Abdali District
Opening Times: Daily, 10:00 AM - 10:00 PM
Friday Market Location: Downtown Amman
Opening Times: Fridays, 8:00 AM - 6:00 PM

Amman's Modern Side

While Amman is steeped in history, it is also a city that embraces modernity. The city has a burgeoning tech scene, and areas like Abdali are testament to this transformation. The Abdali Boulevard, for instance, is a new downtown area with sleek architecture, luxury hotels, and high-end retail spaces.

Location: Abdali District, Amman
Opening Times: Most establishments are open daily, 10:00 AM - late night

Practical Information

When visiting Amman, it's essential to be aware of local customs and etiquette. Jordanians are known for their hospitality, and you'll often be invited to share a cup of tea or coffee. Dress modestly, especially when visiting religious sites. Taxis are a common mode of transportation in Amman, and it's advisable to agree on a fare before starting your journey, as meters are not always used.

Petra

The Entrance and the Siq

Your journey into Petra begins at the Visitor Center, located at the entrance of the site in Wadi Musa. Open from 6:00 AM to 6:00 PM in the summer and 6:00 AM to 4:00 PM in the winter, this is where you can purchase your tickets, hire a guide, or pick up a map. From here, you'll walk down a gently sloping path towards the Siq, a narrow gorge that serves as the main entrance to Petra.

The Siq is a natural geological wonder, stretching for about 1.2 kilometers with towering cliffs on either side. As you walk through the Siq, you'll notice the remains of ancient carvings and water channels that once supplied the city. The path twists and turns, creating a sense of anticipation as you approach the city's main attraction.

The Treasury (Al-Khazneh)

Emerging from the Siq, you'll be greeted by the breathtaking sight of Al-Khazneh, or the Treasury. Carved directly into the sandstone cliff, the Treasury is an architectural marvel that dates back to the 1st century AD. Its elaborate façade, adorned with intricate carvings and Corinthian columns, is instantly recognizable.

Despite its name, the Treasury was not a depository for riches. Instead, it is believed to have been a royal tomb or a temple. Spend some time marveling at the detailed craftsmanship and take in the grandeur of this iconic structure. Early morning and late afternoon are the best times to visit, as the sunlight casts a golden glow on the façade, enhancing its beauty.

The Street of Facades and the Theater

Continuing your exploration, you'll come across the Street of Facades. This area is lined with numerous tombs and houses carved into the rock face. Each structure has its own unique design, reflecting the wealth and status of its original inhabitants.

Nearby, you'll find the Theater, a grand amphitheater that could seat up to 8,500 people. Carved into the mountainside, the Theater offers a glimpse into the entertainment and social life of the Nabataeans, the ancient people who built Petra. Climb to the upper tiers for a panoramic view of the surrounding area.

The Royal Tombs

A short walk from the Theater leads you to the Royal Tombs, a series of large and elaborate tombs cut into the cliffs. Among these, the Urn Tomb stands out with its grand colonnaded terrace. The Silk Tomb, with its swirling colors, and the Corinthian Tomb, with its intricate carvings, are also worth exploring. Each tomb tells a story of the city's past and the people who once lived there.

The Colonnaded Street and the Great Temple

As you continue deeper into Petra, you'll arrive at the Colonnaded Street, the main thoroughfare of the ancient city. Flanked by columns on either side, this street once bustled with merchants and traders. Today, you can still see the remnants of shops and public buildings that lined the street.

At the end of the Colonnaded Street stands the Great Temple. Covering an area of nearly 7,560 square meters, the Great Temple was a major center of religious and political life in Petra. Take time to explore the temple's expansive courtyards, staircases, and chambers, imagining the grandeur of its heyday.

The Monastery (Ad-Deir)

One of Petra's most impressive and challenging sites to visit is the Monastery, or Ad-Deir. To reach the Monastery, you'll need to climb approximately 800 steps, a trek that takes around 45 minutes to an hour. The effort is well worth it. The Monastery is larger than the Treasury and equally as stunning, with a massive façade and expansive views of the surrounding landscape.

Pack plenty of water and take breaks as needed during your climb. Once you reach the top, you can relax at a nearby café, enjoy the view, and take in the majesty of the Monastery. It's an experience you won't soon forget.

Petra by Night
For a truly magical experience, consider visiting Petra by Night. This event takes place on Mondays, Wednesdays, and Thursdays, starting at 8:30 PM. The path to the Treasury is lit by thousands of candles, creating an ethereal atmosphere. As you sit in front of the Treasury, you'll be treated to traditional Bedouin music and storytelling, offering a unique perspective on this ancient city.

Practical Tips for Visiting Petra
To make the most of your visit to Petra, here are some practical tips:

Wear Comfortable Footwear: You'll be doing a lot of walking, so sturdy, comfortable shoes are a must.

Stay Hydrated: Carry plenty of water, especially if you're visiting during the hotter months.

Protect Yourself from the Sun: Wear a hat, sunglasses, and sunscreen to protect yourself from the sun's rays.

Hire a Guide: To gain deeper insights into Petra's history and significance, consider hiring a local guide. They can provide valuable context and point out details you might otherwise miss.

Start Early: Arriving early in the morning helps you avoid the crowds and the heat, allowing for a more enjoyable experience.

Be Respectful: Remember that Petra is a UNESCO World Heritage Site. Respect the rules, avoid climbing on the monuments, and do not remove any artifacts.

Wadi Rum

The Magnificent Landscape
Wadi Rum's unique landscape is characterized by its towering rock formations and sweeping desert plains. These formations, carved by natural forces over millions of years, create a breathtaking panorama. The Seven Pillars of Wisdom, named after T.E. Lawrence's famous book, is one of the most notable rock formations in Wadi Rum. As you explore, you will encounter numerous arches, canyons, and cliffs, each more impressive than the last.

Bedouin Culture and Hospitality
The Bedouins, indigenous people of the desert, have lived in Wadi Rum for centuries. Their culture and traditions are an integral part of the Wadi Rum experience. Visitors have the opportunity to stay in Bedouin camps, where they can enjoy traditional meals, listen to Bedouin music, and learn about their way of life. The Bedouins are known for their hospitality, and staying with them offers a unique chance to experience their warm and welcoming culture firsthand.

Activities and Adventures
Wadi Rum is a playground for adventure enthusiasts. The desert offers a variety of activities that cater to different interests and fitness levels.

Jeep Tours
One of the most popular ways to explore Wadi Rum is by taking a jeep tour. These tours, led by experienced Bedouin guides, take you deep into the desert, allowing you to see the most famous landmarks and hidden gems. You will visit places like the Khazali Canyon, known for its ancient rock inscriptions, and the Burdah Rock Bridge, one of the highest natural arches in the world.

Camel Trekking
For a more traditional experience, consider embarking on a camel trek. Camels, often referred to as the "ships of the desert," have been used by

Bedouins for centuries. Riding a camel through the vast expanse of Wadi Rum gives you a sense of what life in the desert was like in the past. Most camel treks are guided by Bedouins who share their knowledge of the desert and its history.

Rock Climbing and Hiking

Wadi Rum is a paradise for rock climbers and hikers. The towering sandstone cliffs offer routes for all levels of climbers, from beginners to experts. The Jebel Rum, the highest peak in the area, is a popular destination for climbers. Hiking trails, such as the one leading to the summit of Jebel Umm ad Dami, the highest point in Jordan, offer stunning views of the desert landscape.

Hot Air Balloon Rides

For a bird's-eye view of Wadi Rum, consider taking a hot air balloon ride. Floating above the desert at sunrise is a magical experience, offering a unique perspective on the stunning rock formations and vast sandy plains. Balloon rides typically last for about an hour and provide ample opportunities for photography.

Lawrence of Arabia

Wadi Rum is closely associated with T.E. Lawrence, also known as Lawrence of Arabia. Lawrence, a British officer, played a key role in the Arab Revolt against the Ottoman Empire during World War I. His exploits in the desert are legendary, and many sites in Wadi Rum are linked to his story. The Lawrence Spring, a freshwater spring where Lawrence is said to have washed during his travels, is one such site. Another notable location is the Lawrence House, a small rock formation where Lawrence supposedly took shelter.

Stargazing

The clear desert skies of Wadi Rum make it one of the best places for stargazing. Far from the light pollution of cities, the night sky in Wadi Rum is a canvas of stars. Many Bedouin camps offer stargazing experiences, where you can relax by the campfire and gaze at the Milky

Way. Some camps even provide telescopes for a closer look at celestial objects.

Practical Information
Getting There
Wadi Rum is located about 60 kilometers east of Aqaba and 320 kilometers south of Amman. The easiest way to reach Wadi Rum is by car. You can rent a car in Aqaba or Amman and drive to the Wadi Rum Visitor Center. Alternatively, you can take a bus or a taxi from Aqaba. The drive from Aqaba to Wadi Rum takes approximately one hour, while the drive from Amman takes around four hours.

Visitor Center
The Wadi Rum Visitor Center is the starting point for all visitors. Here, you will pay the entrance fee (usually around 5 Jordanian Dinars) and arrange for a guide or a jeep tour if you haven't booked one in advance. The visitor center also provides maps and information about the area.

Accommodation
There are several accommodation options in Wadi Rum, ranging from traditional Bedouin camps to luxury desert resorts. Staying in a Bedouin camp is highly recommended for an authentic experience. Camps typically offer tents with basic amenities, shared bathrooms, and communal dining areas. Some popular camps include:

Rum Stars Camp (Coordinates: 29.5343° N, 35.4112° E)
Bedouin Directions Camp (Coordinates: 29.5460° N, 35.4085° E)
Wadi Rum Night Luxury Camp (Coordinates: 29.5746° N, 35.4010° E)
For those seeking more comfort, luxury desert resorts such as the Sun City Camp and the Memories Aicha Luxury Camp offer upscale amenities, including private tents with en-suite bathrooms, air conditioning, and gourmet dining.

Best Time to Visit
The best time to visit Wadi Rum is during the spring (March to May) and autumn (September to November) months when the weather is mild and

pleasant. Summers can be extremely hot, with temperatures often exceeding 40°C (104°F), while winters can be cold, especially at night. Regardless of the season, it is essential to bring appropriate clothing, including layers for the chilly nights, and plenty of sunscreen and water.

Safety Tips
Always travel with a guide or as part of an organized tour.
Carry plenty of water and stay hydrated.
Wear appropriate clothing and footwear for the desert environment.
Be mindful of wildlife and respect the natural environment.
Follow the advice and instructions of your guide at all times.

Dead Sea

Geography and Climate
The Dead Sea is a landlocked salt lake bordered by Jordan to the east and Israel and Palestine to the west. It lies more than 430 meters below sea level, making it the earth's lowest elevation on land. The lake itself is about 50 kilometers long and 15 kilometers wide at its widest point. The climate in this region is arid, with hot summers and mild winters, making it an ideal year-round destination. You'll find that the temperatures here are consistently warmer than in the rest of Jordan, which makes it perfect for a winter getaway.

Therapeutic and Healing Properties
The waters of the Dead Sea are famous for their buoyancy and high mineral content. With a salinity of over 30%, you'll effortlessly float on its surface. The mineral-rich mud found along its shores is believed to have therapeutic benefits, helping to alleviate conditions such as psoriasis, eczema, and arthritis. Visitors often cover themselves in the black mud before taking a dip, and many resorts in the area offer spa treatments that utilize these natural resources.

Major Attractions

Amman Beach

One of the most popular public beaches on the Jordanian side of the Dead Sea, Amman Beach is equipped with various amenities including swimming pools, showers, and restaurants. It's a great place to relax, swim, and enjoy the unique experience of floating in the Dead Sea. The beach is open daily from 8 AM to 6 PM. Address: Amman Beach, Dead Sea, Jordan.

Dead Sea Panoramic Complex

For stunning views of the Dead Sea and beyond, visit the Dead Sea Panoramic Complex. Located on a cliff edge, this complex offers a museum, a restaurant, and several viewpoints where you can enjoy breathtaking vistas. The museum provides an informative overview of the Dead Sea's geological and ecological significance. Opening hours: 9 AM to 7 PM. Address: Dead Sea Highway, Dead Sea, Jordan.

Ma'in Hot Springs

Located near the Dead Sea, Ma'in Hot Springs is a series of hot mineral springs and waterfalls. The thermal waters are rich in minerals and are believed to have therapeutic benefits. There are several pools and a spa resort where you can enjoy the warm waters and relax in a serene setting. Address: Ma'in Hot Springs, Dead Sea, Jordan.

Mujib Nature Reserve

For those seeking adventure, the Mujib Nature Reserve offers hiking trails that cater to various levels of difficulty. The Siq Trail, in particular, is a popular route that takes you through a stunning gorge with waterfalls and natural pools. The reserve is home to diverse wildlife and offers a unique perspective on the natural beauty surrounding the Dead Sea. Opening hours: 8 AM to 3 PM. Address: Mujib Nature Reserve, Dead Sea, Jordan.

Historical and Cultural Significance

The Dead Sea region is steeped in history and biblical significance. It is believed to be the site of the ancient cities of Sodom and Gomorrah, mentioned in the Bible. Nearby, the archaeological site of Bethany

Beyond the Jordan (Al-Maghtas) is considered the place where John the Baptist baptized Jesus. This UNESCO World Heritage Site is a must-visit for its historical and religious importance. Address: Bethany Beyond the Jordan, Dead Sea, Jordan. Opening hours: 8 AM to 5 PM.

Accommodation and Dining
You'll find a range of accommodation options along the Jordanian side of the Dead Sea, from luxury resorts to budget-friendly hotels.

Kempinski Hotel Ishtar Dead Sea
A luxurious resort offering stunning views of the Dead Sea, the Kempinski Hotel Ishtar features multiple pools, a private beach, and world-class spa facilities. It's an ideal choice for those looking to indulge in luxury while enjoying the therapeutic benefits of the Dead Sea. Address: Sweimeh, Dead Sea Road, Dead Sea, Jordan.

Dead Sea Marriott Resort & Spa
This resort offers a perfect blend of comfort and luxury with its spacious rooms, several dining options, and a variety of recreational activities. The on-site spa provides treatments using Dead Sea mud and salts, enhancing your relaxation experience. Address: Dead Sea Road, Sweimeh, Dead Sea, Jordan.

Crowne Plaza Jordan - Dead Sea Resort & Spa
A family-friendly resort that caters to all age groups with its multiple pools, kids' club, and a wide range of dining options. The spa offers treatments utilizing the natural resources of the Dead Sea. Address: Dead Sea Road, Sweimeh, Dead Sea, Jordan.
For dining, many of these resorts offer restaurants that serve a variety of cuisines, from traditional Jordanian dishes to international fare. You'll have the opportunity to enjoy meals with stunning views of the Dead Sea.

Aqaba

Beaches and Water Activities

Aqaba's beaches are one of its biggest draws. The city boasts several public and private beaches where you can enjoy the sun and sea. The Berenice Beach Club, located at South Beach, is a popular choice. Here, you can relax on the sandy shore, take a dip in the sea, or enjoy a range of water activities. The club offers facilities like pools, a restaurant, and a diving center. It is located 13 kilometers south of Aqaba's city center.

Diving and snorkeling are must-do activities in Aqaba. The Red Sea is renowned for its vibrant coral reefs and diverse marine life. You can explore these underwater wonders at sites like the Japanese Garden, Cedar Pride Shipwreck, and the Seven Sisters. Several dive centers in Aqaba, such as the Aqaba Adventure Divers (South Beach Road), offer guided dives and courses for all levels. Most dive centers are open daily from early morning until late afternoon.

Historical and Cultural Sites

Aqaba is steeped in history, and you can explore this rich past through its many historical sites. Start with the Aqaba Fort, also known as Mamluk Castle, located in the city center. The fort, originally built in the 14th century, has been rebuilt and renovated over the centuries. It offers a glimpse into the region's military history and provides stunning views of the Gulf of Aqaba.

Adjacent to the fort is the Aqaba Archaeological Museum. The museum houses artifacts dating back to the Bronze Age, showcasing the city's long and varied history. Highlights include pottery, coins, and inscriptions. The museum is located at Raghadan Street and is open daily from 8:00 AM to 4:00 PM.

Another significant site is the Ayla Oasis. Ayla was an ancient Islamic city and an important trade center. Today, the archaeological site reveals remnants of early Islamic architecture. You can stroll through the ruins and imagine life in Aqaba centuries ago. Ayla is located near the city center, close to the marina.

Modern Attractions

For a more contemporary experience, visit the Aqaba Marine Park. This park is dedicated to preserving the marine environment of the Red Sea while offering recreational activities. You can snorkel, dive, or take a glass-bottom boat tour to see the colorful coral reefs and marine life. The park also has educational facilities where you can learn about marine conservation efforts. The Aqaba Marine Park is located along the coast, south of the city center.

The Aqaba Bird Observatory is another modern attraction worth visiting. This site is a haven for bird watchers, as it attracts a wide variety of migratory birds. The observatory is located near the Jordanian-Israeli border and is best visited during the spring and autumn migration seasons.

Dining and Nightlife

Aqaba's culinary scene is diverse, offering everything from traditional Jordanian cuisine to international dishes. For a taste of local flavors, head to Al-Shami Restaurant, located at Al-Razi Street. This restaurant is known for its delicious mezze, fresh seafood, and traditional Jordanian dishes like mansaf. It's a great place to enjoy a meal in a lively, family-friendly atmosphere.

For a more upscale dining experience, visit the Royal Yacht Club Restaurant. This waterfront restaurant offers stunning views of the marina and serves a range of seafood and Mediterranean dishes. It's located at the Royal Yacht Club, King Hussein Street, and is open daily from noon to midnight.

Aqaba's nightlife is relatively low-key but enjoyable. Many hotels and beach clubs offer evening entertainment, such as live music and traditional dance performances. The Kempinski Hotel Aqaba Red Sea (King Hussein Street) and the Movenpick Resort & Residences Aqaba (King Hussein Street) are known for their vibrant nightlife scenes.

Shopping

Shopping in Aqaba is a blend of traditional and modern experiences. The Aqaba City Center Mall (King Hussein Street) offers a variety of shops, including international brands, local boutiques, and a supermarket. It's a convenient place to shop for souvenirs, clothing, and essentials.

For a more traditional shopping experience, visit the Aqaba Souk. Located in the heart of the city, the souk is a bustling marketplace where you can find everything from spices and textiles to handicrafts and jewelry. It's a great place to haggle for unique souvenirs and immerse yourself in the local culture.

Accommodation

Aqaba offers a range of accommodation options to suit different budgets and preferences. For a luxurious stay, consider the InterContinental Aqaba Resort, located at King Hussein Street. This five-star resort features a private beach, multiple pools, and several dining options. It's a perfect choice for those seeking comfort and elegance.

For mid-range options, the Captain's Hotel (Al Nahda Street) provides comfortable rooms, a rooftop terrace, and a restaurant serving local and international cuisine. It's a popular choice among families and couples looking for a pleasant stay at an affordable price.

Budget travelers can opt for the Bedouin Garden Village, located at South Beach. This budget-friendly hotel offers basic but comfortable rooms, a pool, and easy access to the beach and dive sites. It's an excellent choice for those who want to experience Aqaba's natural beauty without breaking the bank.

Excursions and Day Trips

Aqaba is an excellent base for exploring the surrounding region. One of the most popular day trips is to the Wadi Rum Desert. Known as the Valley of the Moon, Wadi Rum offers stunning desert landscapes, towering rock formations, and ancient petroglyphs. You can take a jeep tour, go hiking, or spend a night in a Bedouin camp under the stars. Wadi Rum is about an hour's drive from Aqaba.

Another great excursion is a trip to the ancient city of Petra. This UNESCO World Heritage Site is one of Jordan's most famous attractions. From Aqaba, you can take a guided tour or drive to Petra, which is about a two-hour journey. Spend the day exploring the rock-cut architecture, tombs, and temples of this incredible archaeological site.

Practical Information
Aqaba is well-connected to the rest of Jordan and neighboring countries. The King Hussein International Airport (located 10 kilometers north of the city) offers flights to major cities in the region. There are also regular bus services connecting Aqaba to Amman, Petra, and other destinations within Jordan.
Getting around Aqaba is easy, with taxis being the most common mode of transport. You can also rent a car if you prefer to explore the region at your own pace. The city center is compact and walkable, making it convenient to explore on foot.

Jerash

Located in the northern part of Jordan, approximately 48 kilometers north of the capital city Amman, Jerash is one of the country's most impressive historical sites. Known for its well-preserved Greco-Roman architecture, the city offers a fascinating glimpse into the past, attracting thousands of tourists every year.

Historical Significance
Jerash, also known as Gerasa in ancient times, is renowned for its extensive and well-preserved ruins of a once-thriving Roman city. The city dates back more than 6,500 years and became a significant trading center during the Roman period. The ruins reflect Jerash's importance and wealth during its peak.

The Jerash Archaeological Museum
Begin your journey through Jerash at the Jerash Archaeological Museum. Located at the entrance of the site, the museum houses a collection of artifacts found in Jerash and the surrounding areas. The exhibits include pottery, coins, statues, and mosaics that provide insight

into the city's history and daily life during ancient times. The museum is open daily from 8:00 AM to 4:00 PM.
Address: Entrance of the Jerash ruins, Jerash, Jordan
Location: Jerash Governorate, northern Jordan

The Oval Plaza
One of Jerash's most iconic landmarks is the Oval Plaza, a massive elliptical forum surrounded by 56 Ionic columns. The plaza serves as a central point of the ancient city, where public gatherings and events took place. Standing in the middle of the plaza, you can imagine the bustling activity of the Roman marketplace.
Location: Center of the Jerash ruins, Jerash, Jordan

The Cardo Maximus
Stretching over 800 meters, the Cardo Maximus is the main street of Jerash. This colonnaded avenue was the heart of the city's commercial and social life. As you walk along the well-preserved stone pavement, you'll notice the grooves left by ancient chariot wheels, adding a tangible sense of history. The street is lined with columns and the remnants of shops, fountains, and public buildings.
Location: Runs through the center of the Jerash ruins, Jerash, Jordan

The North Theater
Constructed in 165 AD, the North Theater is one of two Roman theaters in Jerash. Originally used for city council meetings, it later became a venue for performances. The theater could accommodate up to 1,600 spectators and is still used today for the Jerash Festival of Culture and Arts, which features performances by local and international artists.
Location: Northern part of the Jerash ruins, Jerash, Jordan

The South Theater
The South Theater, larger than its northern counterpart, could seat more than 3,000 people. Built in the 1st century AD, it remains an impressive sight with its well-preserved stage and seating area. The theater offers excellent acoustics, allowing even a whisper to be heard throughout the auditorium.

Location: Southern part of the Jerash ruins, Jerash, Jordan

The Temple of Artemis
Dedicated to the patron goddess of Jerash, the Temple of Artemis is another must-see site. Built in the 2nd century AD, the temple's grand columns and intricate carvings highlight the architectural prowess of the Romans. Although partially in ruins, the temple's grandeur is still evident.
Location: Northern part of the Jerash ruins, Jerash, Jordan

The Nymphaeum
The Nymphaeum, a monumental public fountain, is another highlight of Jerash. Built in 191 AD, it was dedicated to the nymphs and adorned with elaborate carvings and statues. Water once cascaded from the fountain into a large pool, providing a refreshing spot for residents and visitors.
Location: Along the Cardo Maximus, Jerash, Jordan

Hadrian's Arch
Erected in 130 AD to honor Emperor Hadrian's visit to Jerash, Hadrian's Arch stands as a grand entrance to the ancient city. The arch is an impressive example of Roman triumphal architecture and marks the beginning of your journey into the city's past.
Location: Southern entrance of the Jerash ruins, Jerash, Jordan

The Hippodrome
The Hippodrome, a Roman circus used for chariot races and other spectacles, is a testament to Jerash's vibrant entertainment culture. The arena could hold up to 15,000 spectators and remains one of the best-preserved hippodromes in the region. Visitors can witness reenactments of Roman chariot races and gladiator battles, offering a unique glimpse into ancient entertainment.
Location: Eastern part of the Jerash ruins, Jerash, Jordan

Ajloun Castle
A short drive from Jerash, Ajloun Castle offers stunning views of the surrounding countryside. Built in the 12th century by the Ayyubids, the

castle was a strategic fortress against the Crusaders. Today, it provides an excellent vantage point to appreciate the natural beauty and historical significance of the region.

Address: Ajloun Governorate, northern Jordan
Location: 16 kilometers west of Jerash, Jordan

The Jerash Festival of Culture and Arts

Held annually, the Jerash Festival of Culture and Arts transforms the ancient city into a vibrant cultural hub. The festival features performances in music, dance, theater, and poetry by artists from around the world. The festival provides a unique opportunity to experience the rich cultural heritage of Jordan amidst the backdrop of its historical ruins.

Location: Jerash ruins, Jerash, Jordan
Time: Annually, typically in July or August

Local Cuisine

Exploring Jerash wouldn't be complete without savoring the local cuisine. The city offers a variety of dining options where you can enjoy traditional Jordanian dishes such as mansaf, a lamb dish cooked in yogurt, and maqluba, a flavorful rice dish with meat and vegetables. For a more immersive experience, visit a local restaurant where you can enjoy your meal with a view of the ancient ruins.

Madaba

St. George's Church and the Madaba Map

Your journey in Madaba should start at St. George's Church, home to the famous Madaba Map. This Greek Orthodox Church, located at K. Talal St. 30, Madaba, is renowned for its 6th-century mosaic map of Jerusalem and the Holy Land. The map, made from over two million pieces of colored stone, is the oldest surviving original cartographic depiction of the Holy Land and depicts significant biblical sites. Visiting hours are from 8:00 AM to 5:00 PM daily. As you stand before the map, imagine the meticulous craftsmanship that went into its creation and consider how it has guided pilgrims over the centuries.

Archaeological Park
A short walk from St. George's Church is the Madaba Archaeological Park, an open-air museum that showcases a collection of stunning mosaics from different historical periods. Located on Al-Mahaba Street, this park houses the remnants of Roman, Byzantine, and Islamic buildings, including the Church of the Virgin and the Hippolytus Hall. The highlight is the vibrant mosaics, each telling a story of the city's rich cultural tapestry. The park is open from 8:00 AM to 5:00 PM, offering ample time to explore and appreciate the artistry of ancient civilizations.

Church of the Apostles
Another notable site is the Church of the Apostles, found on Abu Bakr Al Siddiq Street. This 6th-century church is known for its intricate mosaic floor, particularly the depiction of Thalassa, the goddess of the sea, surrounded by marine life. The vivid colors and detailed designs are a testament to the high level of craftsmanship achieved by ancient mosaic artists. The church is open from 8:00 AM to 5:00 PM, and as you walk through, you can almost hear the whispers of the past and the stories these stones have witnessed.

Madaba Museum
To gain a comprehensive understanding of Madaba's history, a visit to the Madaba Museum is essential. Located near the city center on Al-Jaheth Street, this museum houses artifacts from various periods, including the Bronze Age, Iron Age, and Islamic periods. You will find pottery, coins, and other archaeological finds that paint a vivid picture of life in ancient Madaba. The museum is open from 8:00 AM to 4:00 PM. Walking through its halls, you can trace the evolution of the city's culture and its significance through the ages.

Mount Nebo
A short drive from Madaba, Mount Nebo offers a panoramic view that is both breathtaking and historically significant. According to biblical

tradition, this is the place where Moses was granted a view of the Promised Land. At the summit, you'll find the Memorial Church of Moses, built on the remains of a 4th-century monastery. The site, managed by the Franciscan order, is open from 8:00 AM to 5:00 PM. As you stand at the viewpoint, gazing out over the Jordan Valley, the Dead Sea, and even Jerusalem on a clear day, you can reflect on the profound history and spiritual significance of this location.

Machaerus (Mukawir)
Another historical gem near Madaba is Machaerus, known locally as Mukawir. This hilltop fortress, located 25 kilometers southwest of Madaba, is believed to be the site where John the Baptist was imprisoned and executed. The ruins of Herod the Great's palace offer a glimpse into the grandeur of the past. The site is open from 8:00 AM to 4:00 PM. Climbing to the top, you can imagine the events that transpired here and enjoy the sweeping views of the surrounding landscape.

Local Markets and Souks
Madaba's vibrant markets are a great way to immerse yourself in local culture. The main market area, located in the city center, is bustling with activity and offers a variety of goods, from fresh produce to traditional crafts. Here, you can shop for handmade mosaics, ceramics, and other souvenirs that reflect the city's artistic heritage. As you stroll through the market, you'll experience the sights, sounds, and scents that define daily life in Madaba. The market is typically open from early morning until late evening.

Dining in Madaba
No visit to Madaba is complete without sampling its culinary delights. The city boasts a variety of restaurants offering traditional Jordanian cuisine. Haret Jdoudna, located on Talal Street, is a popular choice. Set in a historic building, this restaurant offers a charming atmosphere and serves a range of local dishes, including mansaf, a traditional Jordanian lamb dish. As you dine, you'll appreciate the blend of flavors and the rich culinary traditions of the region. The restaurant is open from 11:00 AM to 11:00 PM.

Chapter 4:

Historical and Cultural Sites

Petra

Entering Petra

Your journey into Petra begins with a walk through the Siq, a narrow, winding gorge approximately 1.2 kilometers long. The Siq, with walls that tower up to 80 meters high, serves as a dramatic gateway to the city. As you make your way through, you'll notice intricate carvings and niches that hint at the Nabataeans' reverence for their gods and ancestors. The Siq itself is a natural geological feature, formed by a split in the sandstone rock, and it sets the stage for the awe-inspiring sight that awaits you at its end.

The Treasury (Al-Khazneh)

Emerging from the Siq, you are greeted by the breathtaking façade of Al-Khazneh, commonly known as the Treasury. This monumental structure, standing at 39 meters high, is a testament to the skill and artistry of the Nabataean craftsmen. Carved directly into the rose-colored rock, the Treasury's ornate façade features a blend of Hellenistic and Nabataean architecture, with Corinthian columns, statues, and friezes. It is believed that the Treasury was originally constructed as a mausoleum for a Nabataean king, though local legends suggest it was used to store treasure.

The Street of Facades

Beyond the Treasury lies the Street of Facades, a broad pathway lined with tombs and houses carved into the rock face. These structures, with their intricate facades, provide a glimpse into the daily lives and burial practices of the Nabataeans. As you stroll along this street, you can imagine the bustling activity that once filled this ancient city, from merchants trading goods to families visiting the tombs of their ancestors.

The Theatre
Continuing your exploration, you will come across the Theatre, a grand amphitheater carved into the mountainside. The Theatre, with a capacity of approximately 8,500 spectators, reflects the influence of Roman architecture and highlights Petra's significance as a cultural and social hub. The seating area, or cavea, offers stunning views of the surrounding tombs and temples, and you can almost hear the echoes of ancient performances and gatherings.

The Royal Tombs
Further along, you will encounter the Royal Tombs, a series of impressive mausoleums that showcase the wealth and power of Petra's elite. The most notable of these tombs are the Urn Tomb, the Silk Tomb, the Corinthian Tomb, and the Palace Tomb. Each of these structures features unique architectural elements and intricate carvings, providing insights into the Nabataeans' funerary customs and artistic achievements. The Urn Tomb, for example, is distinguished by its large urn-shaped finial and a grand courtyard that suggests it may have served as a place of worship.

The Monastery (Ad Deir)
A challenging yet rewarding hike up 800 steps carved into the rock will lead you to the Monastery, or Ad Deir. This massive structure, similar in design to the Treasury but even larger, stands at an impressive 50 meters wide and 45 meters high. The Monastery is believed to have been a Nabataean temple, later repurposed as a Christian monastery during the Byzantine era. The panoramic views from the Monastery's elevated location offer a breathtaking perspective of the Petra basin and the surrounding mountains.

The Great Temple

As you descend from the Monastery, make your way to the Great Temple, one of the largest and most complex structures in Petra. The Great Temple, which covers an area of 7,560 square meters, features a grand staircase, colonnaded courtyards, and a large central hall.

Excavations suggest that the temple was used for both religious and administrative purposes, and its intricate design reflects the Nabataeans' architectural prowess and their ability to adapt Hellenistic styles to their unique context.

The Petra Church
The Petra Church, also known as the Byzantine Church, is another significant site that highlights Petra's long history of religious diversity. This early Christian basilica, constructed in the 5th or 6th century AD, features beautifully preserved mosaic floors depicting scenes of nature and daily life. The church's remains include three apses, a nave, and a series of rooms that may have served as a bishop's residence. The Petra Church offers a fascinating glimpse into the transition from pagan to Christian worship in the region.

The High Place of Sacrifice
For those seeking a more adventurous exploration, the High Place of Sacrifice offers a unique perspective on Petra's religious practices. This sacred site, located on a mountain summit, requires a steep climb but rewards you with stunning panoramic views of the city below. The High Place of Sacrifice features two obelisks and a large altar, where animals were likely sacrificed to the Nabataean gods. The surrounding area also includes rock-cut cisterns and other ceremonial structures, adding to the site's historical and cultural significance.

Petra by Night
To experience Petra in a different light, consider attending Petra by Night, an event that takes place on select evenings. As you walk through the Siq and approach the Treasury, the path is illuminated by thousands of candles, creating a magical and almost otherworldly atmosphere. The evening includes a traditional Bedouin music performance and

storytelling session, allowing you to immerse yourself in the rich cultural heritage of the Nabataeans. Petra by Night offers a unique opportunity to see the Rose City in a new and enchanting way.

Practical Information
Location: Petra is located in the Ma'an Governorate, approximately 240 kilometers south of Amman, Jordan's capital. The site is easily accessible by car, bus, or organized tour.

Opening Hours: Petra is open daily from 6:00 AM to 6:00 PM during the summer months (April to October) and from 6:00 AM to 4:00 PM during the winter months (November to March). Petra by Night takes place on Mondays, Wednesdays, and Thursdays, starting at 8:30 PM and ending at 10:30 PM.

Admission Fees: The entrance fee for Petra varies depending on the length of your visit. A one-day ticket costs 50 Jordanian Dinars (JOD), a two-day ticket costs 55 JOD, and a three-day ticket costs 60 JOD. Tickets for Petra by Night are sold separately and cost 17 JOD.

Address: Petra, Wadi Musa, Ma'an Governorate, Jordan.
Visiting Petra is an unforgettable experience, offering a deep dive into the rich history and culture of the Nabataeans.

Jerash

When you visit Jordan, a trip to the ancient city of Jerash is an absolute must. Known as the "Pompeii of the East," Jerash is one of the best-preserved Roman provincial towns in the world. Located approximately 48 kilometers (30 miles) north of Amman, Jerash offers an unparalleled glimpse into the grandeur of Roman urban life.
As you approach the site, you'll pass through the modern city of Jerash before reaching the main entrance to the archaeological park. The address is Jerash Archaeological Park, Wasfi Al-Tal Street, Jerash,

Jordan. The park is typically open from 8:00 AM to 4:00 PM in the winter and 8:00 AM to 6:00 PM in the summer, though these times can vary slightly.

Entering the archaeological park, you'll immediately be struck by the magnitude of the ruins. The city's history stretches back over 6,500 years, but it was under Roman rule that Jerash, then known as Gerasa, flourished. The grandeur of the Roman architecture, with its temples, theaters, and colonnaded streets, transports you back in time.

Start your exploration at the **South Gate**, the main entrance to the ancient city. As you pass through the gate, imagine the bustling activity of traders, soldiers, and citizens who once passed through these same stone arches.

Next, you'll encounter the **Hippodrome**, a massive sports arena that once seated up to 15,000 spectators. It was here that chariot races, athletic contests, and other public events were held. Standing in the center of the Hippodrome, you can almost hear the roar of the crowd and the thunder of hooves on the stone track.

From the Hippodrome, make your way to the **Oval Plaza**, a unique and iconic feature of Jerash. This large, oval-shaped forum is surrounded by a colonnade of 56 Ionic columns and was the focal point of public life in ancient Gerasa. The plaza's design is both grand and harmonious, offering a perfect spot for capturing stunning photographs.

Adjacent to the Oval Plaza is the **Cardo Maximus**, the main street of the city. This colonnaded avenue stretches for over 800 meters and was lined with shops, public buildings, and fountains. Walking along the Cardo, you'll notice the ruts worn into the stone by ancient carts, a testament to the city's vibrant commercial activity.

As you continue along the Cardo, you'll come across the **South Theatre**, one of the most impressive structures in Jerash. This large amphitheater could seat around 3,000 people and was used for various performances and public meetings. Climbing to the top tier of seats provides a panoramic view of the ancient city, offering a sense of the scale and grandeur of the Roman urban planning.

Another highlight is the **Temple of Artemis**, dedicated to the city's patron goddess. The temple's massive columns, some still standing at over 13 meters high, give an idea of the structure's original magnificence. The temple complex includes a grand staircase and a spacious courtyard, where religious ceremonies were once held.

Nearby, you'll find the **North Theatre**, smaller than the South Theatre but equally impressive. This theater was used mainly for city council meetings and smaller performances. Its well-preserved seating and stage area allow you to imagine the political and cultural discussions that took place here.

One of the most awe-inspiring sites in Jerash is the **Nymphaeum**, a monumental public fountain dedicated to the nymphs. This elaborate structure, adorned with carvings and mosaics, served as both a public water source and a decorative feature. The water, which once flowed from its many spouts, would have been a welcome sight for the city's inhabitants.

Your tour of Jerash would be incomplete without visiting the **Arch of Hadrian**, built to honor the visit of Emperor Hadrian in 129 AD. This triumphal arch stands at the entrance to the city and marks the start of the Cardo Maximus. Its grandeur is a fitting testament to the city's importance during Roman times.

Throughout your visit, you'll notice that Jerash is not just a collection of ruins but a living testament to the past. The city's layout, with its grid of streets, public spaces, and buildings, provides a clear picture of Roman urban planning. The preservation of these structures allows you to walk the same streets and visit the same buildings that citizens of Gerasa did nearly two millennia ago.

Imagine standing in the Oval Plaza, surrounded by the towering columns, as the sun sets and casts long shadows across the stone pavement. The air is filled with the sounds of modern-day Jerash mingling with the echoes of history. You can almost see the ancient marketplace, bustling with merchants and shoppers, and hear the distant cheers from the Hippodrome.

As you explore Jerash, you might also encounter local artisans selling souvenirs, traditional crafts, and refreshments near the main entrance and within the archaeological park. These vendors offer a glimpse into the modern culture of Jordan, providing a connection between the past and present.

In addition to the main archaeological sites, consider visiting the **Jerash Archaeological Museum**, located within the park. The museum houses a collection of artifacts discovered during excavations, including pottery, coins, statues, and jewelry. These items offer further insight into the daily life and culture of ancient Gerasa.

Your visit to Jerash is not just a journey through time but also an opportunity to experience the rich history and cultural heritage of Jordan. The city's well-preserved ruins, combined with its scenic location and welcoming atmosphere, make it a highlight of any trip to Jordan.

Amman Citadel and Roman Theatre

Amman Citadel

Perched atop Jabal al-Qal'a, one of the seven hills that originally made up Amman, the Amman Citadel offers panoramic views of the city and an insight into its historical layers. The Citadel is home to various ruins, each telling a story from different eras, including the Roman, Byzantine, and Umayyad periods.

One of the most striking features of the Citadel is the Temple of Hercules. Built during the reign of Emperor Marcus Aurelius (AD 161–180), the temple's massive columns are visible from various points in Amman, making it a prominent symbol of the city's Roman past. The partially reconstructed pillars and the scattered remnants around them give you a sense of the temple's former grandeur.

Nearby, you'll find the Umayyad Palace, dating back to the early Islamic period around AD 720. The palace complex includes a large audience hall with a domed entrance chamber that has been partially restored. Walking through the remnants of the palace, you can imagine the administrative and ceremonial activities that once took place here.

The Byzantine Church, also located within the Citadel, provides a stark contrast to the Islamic and Roman structures surrounding it. This basilica, dating back to the 6th or 7th century, showcases the early Christian influence in the region. The mosaic floors and the remaining stone columns offer a glimpse into the architectural style of that era.

For a deeper understanding of the Citadel's significance, visit the Jordan Archaeological Museum situated on the site. Established in 1951, the museum houses artifacts from various Jordanian archaeological sites, ranging from prehistoric times to the 15th century. Notable exhibits include the Dead Sea Scrolls, a collection of pottery, and a series of statues dating back to the Neolithic period, providing context to the Citadel's historical importance.

The Citadel is open to visitors daily from 8:00 AM to 5:00 PM in winter and from 8:00 AM to 7:00 PM in summer. It is located at K. Ali Ben Al-Hussein St. 146, Amman, and is easily accessible by taxi or local transportation. Spending a few hours here allows you to traverse through centuries of history and gain a comprehensive understanding of Amman's evolution.

Roman Theatre

Located at the foot of Jabal al-Joufah, in the heart of downtown Amman, the Roman Theatre is another must-visit historical site. Built during the reign of Antonius Pius (AD 138–161), the theatre is an impressive structure that highlights the architectural prowess of the Romans. With a seating capacity of 6,000, the theatre was designed to host performances and public events, demonstrating the cultural life of ancient Philadelphia (the ancient name of Amman).

The theatre is divided into three horizontal sections, known as diazomata, which provided different levels of seating. The first level, closest to the stage, was reserved for the city's elite, while the upper levels were for the general public. The steep seating arrangement ensures excellent acoustics, allowing sound to travel efficiently throughout the amphitheatre.

As you walk through the theatre, imagine the bustling activity that once took place here. The central stage area, known as the orchestra, was used for performances by actors and musicians. The large stage wall, or scaenae frons, behind the orchestra, was adorned with columns and statues, adding to the visual grandeur of the performances.

Adjacent to the Roman Theatre are two smaller museums that provide additional context to the site. The Jordan Folklore Museum, located in the eastern wing of the theatre, showcases traditional Jordanian life, including costumes, tools, and musical instruments.

Meanwhile, the Jordanian Museum of Popular Traditions, housed in the western wing, displays artifacts related to Jordanian and Palestinian heritage, including jewelry, pottery, and mosaics.

The Roman Theatre is open to visitors daily from 8:00 AM to 6:00 PM in summer and from 8:00 AM to 4:00 PM in winter. It is located at Hashemite Plaza, Al-Hashemi Street, Amman. The central location makes it accessible by foot if you're staying in downtown Amman, or by taxi from other parts of the city.

Umm Qais (Gadara)

When visiting Jordan, one of the historical gems you must not miss is Umm Qais, also known as Gadara. This site offers a fascinating blend of ancient ruins, stunning landscapes, and rich history. Located in northern Jordan, Umm Qais stands on a plateau overlooking the Sea of Galilee, the Yarmouk River, and the Golan Heights, providing breathtaking panoramic views that add to its allure.

Historical Significance

Umm Qais, or ancient Gadara, was part of the Decapolis, a group of ten cities on the eastern frontier of the Roman Empire in the southeastern Levant. These cities were centers of Greek and Roman culture in a region that was predominantly Semitic. Gadara was renowned in ancient times for its intellectual life, and it was the birthplace of several notable philosophers and poets, including Menippus, Theodorus, and Meleager. The city was an important cultural hub and contributed significantly to the region's Hellenistic and Roman heritage.

Architectural Highlights

Upon arriving at Umm Qais, one of the first things you'll notice is the well-preserved Roman theater. This black basalt theater, constructed in the second century AD, could seat around 3,000 spectators. As you walk through the site, the meticulous stonework and the acoustics of the theater will transport you back to the days when it hosted dramatic performances and gatherings.

Another notable structure is the colonnaded street, once the main thoroughfare of Gadara. Walking along this street, you can imagine the bustling life of the city, with merchants, locals, and travelers going about their daily routines. The columns, though weathered by time, still stand as a testament to the grandeur of the Roman era.

The Basilica and the Octagonal Church

Umm Qais is also home to several significant Byzantine ruins. The site boasts the remains of a basilica and an octagonal church, both of which highlight the transition from paganism to Christianity in the region. The basilica, with its impressive layout and structure, indicates the importance of Christianity in Gadara during the Byzantine period. The octagonal church, with its unique shape, is an architectural marvel that reflects the innovative spirit of the early Christian builders.

The Ottoman Village

In addition to the ancient ruins, Umm Qais features remnants of an Ottoman-era village. This village, with its quaint stone houses, offers a glimpse into more recent history. You can wander through the narrow streets and imagine the daily life of the villagers who once inhabited these homes. Some of these houses have been restored and repurposed as guesthouses and cafes, providing a charming blend of history and modern hospitality.

The Museum

Located within the Ottoman village is the Umm Qais Museum. This small but informative museum houses a collection of artifacts discovered at the site, including statues, mosaics, and pottery. The museum provides valuable context for the ruins you see around you, helping to piece together the rich tapestry of Umm Qais's history.

Panoramic Views

One of the unique features of Umm Qais is its strategic location, offering panoramic views of the surrounding landscape. From the edge of the plateau, you can see the Sea of Galilee to the northwest, the Golan Heights to the north, and the Yarmouk River to the west. These views not only enhance the beauty of the site but also underscore its historical significance as a crossroads of cultures and civilizations.

Practical Information

Umm Qais is located approximately 110 kilometers north of Amman. It's a drive of about two hours, making it a feasible day trip. The site is open to visitors from 8:00 AM to 6:00 PM in the summer and from 8:00 AM to 4:00 PM in the winter. The entrance fee is minimal, and there are guided tours available if you prefer a more structured visit.

For those who wish to extend their visit, the area around Umm Qais offers several accommodation options, from charming guesthouses to more luxurious hotels. Staying overnight allows you to experience the site at different times of the day, with the early morning and late afternoon light adding a special touch to the ruins.

Nearby Attractions

While Umm Qais itself is a highlight, the surrounding region also offers several attractions worth exploring. The Yarmouk Nature Reserve, located nearby, is an excellent destination for nature lovers. You can enjoy hiking trails, bird watching, and the natural beauty of the Jordan Valley.

Additionally, the town of Irbid, Jordan's second-largest city, is just a short drive away. Irbid offers a range of cultural and historical sites, including the Jordan University of Science and Technology and several museums. The city's lively atmosphere and modern amenities provide a nice contrast to the ancient ruins of Umm Qais.

Dining Options

There are several dining options around Umm Qais. You can enjoy traditional Jordanian cuisine at one of the local restaurants, many of which offer outdoor seating with stunning views. Dishes like mansaf, a traditional Jordanian lamb dish, and mezze platters featuring a variety of appetizers, are must-tries. Dining here provides a perfect way to relax and reflect on the day's explorations.

Desert Castles

Qasr Amra
Location: Approximately 85 kilometers east of Amman, near the village of Amra.
Address: Qasr Amra, Amra, Jordan.
Opening Hours: Daily from 8:00 AM to 4:00 PM; closed on Fridays.
Qasr Amra, a UNESCO World Heritage Site, is perhaps the most renowned of Jordan's desert castles. Built in the early 8th century, this castle is notable for its well-preserved frescoes depicting various scenes of courtly life, animals, and zodiac signs. The castle's architectural design and decorative elements reveal a fusion of Roman, Persian, and local traditions, showcasing the eclectic style of the Umayyad dynasty.
As you wander through Qasr Amra's rooms, you'll notice its bathhouse, a feature that highlights the sophisticated water management and bathing culture of the era. The frescoes on the dome, depicting a celestial scene, are particularly striking and offer insight into the artistic and scientific interests of the Umayyad court.

Qasr al-Kharana
Location: Approximately 60 kilometers east of Amman, situated in the desert.
Address: Qasr al-Kharana, Kharana, Jordan.
Opening Hours: Daily from 8:00 AM to 4:00 PM; closed on Fridays.
Qasr al-Kharana, distinguished by its well-preserved, fortress-like structure, stands out for its imposing walls and towers. Unlike other desert castles, Qasr al-Kharana's design is primarily defensive, reflecting its role as a stronghold or caravanserai. The castle features a series of interconnected rooms and corridors, which served as living quarters, storage areas, and administrative spaces.

The castle's robust architecture and minimalistic decor are indicative of its utilitarian purpose, providing protection for travelers and traders crossing the desert. The strategic placement of Qasr al-Kharana allowed it to control important trade routes and exert influence over the surrounding area.

Qasr al-Hallabat
Location: Approximately 40 kilometers northeast of Amman, near the village of Hallabat.
Address: Qasr al-Hallabat, Hallabat, Jordan.
Opening Hours: Daily from 8:00 AM to 4:00 PM; closed on Fridays.
Qasr al-Hallabat, known for its distinctive blend of Roman and Byzantine architectural elements, stands out among Jordan's desert castles. Originally built as a Roman fort, it was later adapted by the Umayyads into a palace and administrative center. The castle's layout includes a large courtyard, multiple rooms, and a series of baths, all of which reflect the architectural ingenuity of the period.
The site's historical significance is highlighted by its role as a center for the Umayyad administration, serving as a vital link between the eastern desert and the central regions of Jordan. The well-preserved frescoes and inscriptions provide valuable insights into the cultural and administrative practices of the Umayyad era.

Qasr al-Mushatta
Location: Approximately 35 kilometers southeast of Amman, near the town of Mushatta.
Address: Qasr al-Mushatta, Mushatta, Jordan.
Opening Hours: Daily from 8:00 AM to 4:00 PM; closed on Fridays.
Qasr al-Mushatta, though partially ruined, remains one of the most impressive desert castles in Jordan. Its grand scale and intricate carvings reflect the architectural and artistic sophistication of the Umayyad period. The castle's elaborate stonework and decorative motifs showcase a high level of craftsmanship, with influences from both Islamic and pre-Islamic traditions.
The site's historical importance is underscored by its role as a royal palace, providing a glimpse into the opulent lifestyle of the Umayyad

elite. The remnants of the castle's grand hall and courtyards offer a window into the architectural grandeur of the era.

Qasr al-Qastal

Location: Approximately 25 kilometers south of Amman, near the village of Qastal.

Address: Qasr al-Qastal, Qastal, Jordan.

Opening Hours: Daily from 8:00 AM to 4:00 PM; closed on Fridays.

Qasr al-Qastal, situated on the ancient trade route between Arabia and the Levant, served as both a fort and a caravanserai. Its strategic location and robust construction made it a key player in controlling trade and providing hospitality to travelers. The castle's layout includes defensive walls, storage rooms, and living quarters, all designed to withstand the harsh desert conditions.

The architectural features of Qasr al-Qastal highlight its dual purpose as both a fortress and a resting place for travelers. The site's historical significance is evident in its well-preserved structure and its role in the region's trade and defense networks.

Visiting Tips

When visiting Jordan's desert castles, it's essential to prepare for the desert environment. Bring plenty of water, wear sun protection, and be mindful of the often-arid conditions. Most castles have basic amenities, but facilities can be limited, so plan accordingly.

Exploring these ancient sites provides a profound understanding of Jordan's historical and cultural heritage. Each castle offers a unique perspective on the region's past, from its architectural achievements to its strategic importance in the ancient world.

Shobak Castle and Karak Castle

Shobak Castle

Shobak Castle, also known as Montreal Castle, is a significant historical landmark located in southern Jordan. Perched on a hilltop, approximately 20 kilometers northeast of the town of Shobak, the castle offers a glimpse into the rich history and strategic military architecture of the Crusader era. The castle is situated about 110 kilometers south of Amman, making it a manageable day trip from the capital.

Location and Accessibility
The castle is located at coordinates 30.5236° N latitude and 35.6144° E longitude. To reach Shobak Castle from Amman, follow the Desert Highway (Route 15) southward and then take the exit toward Shobak. The road is well-marked, but it is advisable to use a GPS device or a map for precise directions.

Historical Significance
Constructed in the early 12th century by the Crusader King Baldwin I, Shobak Castle served as a crucial stronghold during the Crusades. Its strategic location allowed it to control the key trade routes between the Dead Sea and the Red Sea. The castle's architecture reflects the military ingenuity of its builders, with its circular towers, fortified walls, and a well-designed gatehouse.

During its peak, Shobak Castle was part of a network of fortifications designed to protect the Crusader states from Muslim forces. The castle changed hands several times, ultimately falling into the control of the Muslim leader Salah ad-Din (Saladin) in the late 12th century. The castle was subsequently used by various Muslim rulers until it was abandoned in the 13th century.

Exploring Shobak Castle
Upon arrival, you will find that the castle's imposing walls and towers offer an impressive view of the surrounding landscape. The castle's interior is a maze of rooms, corridors, and chambers that once housed soldiers, administrators, and possibly even prisoners. The well-preserved remains of the cisterns and storage rooms provide insight into the daily life within the fortress.

One of the most striking features of Shobak Castle is its circular tower, which dominates the skyline. Climbing to the top of the tower rewards you with panoramic views of the rugged terrain and the distant desert landscape. As you explore, be sure to visit the castle's chapel, which, despite its ruins, still reveals the castle's religious significance.

Visiting Information
Address: Shobak Castle, Shobak District, Ma'an Governorate, Jordan
Opening Hours: 8:00 AM to 6:00 PM daily
Entrance Fee: Approximately 2 JOD (Jordanian Dinar)

Karak Castle
Karak Castle, situated in the town of Karak, is another must-visit historical site in Jordan. Located approximately 140 kilometers south of Amman, the castle stands on a hilltop overlooking the town and the surrounding plains. Its strategic location and formidable structure make it a key historical site.

Location and Accessibility
Karak Castle is located at coordinates 31.1817° N latitude and 35.7341° E longitude. To get to Karak Castle from Amman, you can take the Desert Highway (Route 15) south, then follow the signs to Karak. The journey takes about two hours by car.

Historical Significance
Karak Castle, like Shobak, was built during the Crusader period. It was constructed by the Crusader King Baldwin I in the early 12th century as a defensive fortification. The castle played a significant role in the Crusades, serving as a key military outpost and administrative center.

The castle's strategic importance is evident from its imposing design. It features massive stone walls, a complex system of underground tunnels, and a series of watchtowers that allowed defenders to monitor the surrounding area. The castle was captured by Salah ad-Din in 1189, following a prolonged siege, and it remained under Muslim control for the remainder of the Crusader period.

Exploring Karak Castle

Karak Castle is renowned for its well-preserved architecture and extensive network of rooms and passageways. As you explore, you will encounter various chambers, including the grand hall, storage rooms, and the castle's impressive gatehouse. The castle's underground tunnels are particularly fascinating, providing a glimpse into the complex defensive mechanisms employed by its builders.

One of the highlights of a visit to Karak Castle is the panoramic view of the town of Karak and the surrounding countryside. From the castle's ramparts, you can enjoy sweeping vistas of the fertile plains and distant mountains.

Visiting Information:

Address: Karak Castle, Karak, Karak Governorate, Jordan

Opening Hours: 8:00 AM to 6:00 PM daily

Entrance Fee: Approximately 2 JOD (Jordanian Dinar)

Chapter 5:

Natural Wonders of Jordan

Wadi Rum Desert

Bedouin Culture

The Bedouins, the indigenous nomadic people of the desert, are an integral part of Wadi Rum's charm. Their lifestyle, deeply intertwined with the desert environment, offers a glimpse into a way of life that has remained largely unchanged for centuries. The Bedouins are renowned for their hospitality, and their rich traditions provide an authentic cultural experience for visitors.

When you visit Wadi Rum, you'll have the opportunity to interact with the Bedouins, often through guided tours or overnight stays in traditional Bedouin camps. These camps, set up in the heart of the desert, offer a glimpse into traditional Bedouin life. You'll find tents made of goat hair, traditional woven rugs, and the simple yet functional furnishings typical of Bedouin homes.

One of the highlights of Bedouin culture is their cuisine. Traditional dishes such as **mansaf** (a lamb and rice dish) and **zarb** (a dish cooked in an underground oven) are commonly served to guests. The preparation and presentation of these dishes reflect the Bedouins' deep connection to the land and their hospitality.

Desert Safaris

A visit to Wadi Rum would be incomplete without experiencing a desert safari. These safaris are the best way to explore the vast and varied landscape of the desert, offering a range of options to suit different interests and levels of adventure.

Jeep Safaris

For those seeking a more relaxed exploration, jeep safaris provide an excellent way to see the major landmarks of Wadi Rum. Guided by local Bedouins, these tours typically last between 3 to 6 hours and cover significant sights such as the **Seven Pillars of Wisdom**, **Lawrence's Spring**, and **Khazali Canyon**. Each site holds historical and geological significance, and your guide will share stories and facts that bring the landscape to life.

Camel Treks

Camel treks offer a more traditional way to traverse the desert. Riding a camel, you'll follow ancient trade routes and explore the stunning vistas at a slower pace. These treks can range from a few hours to several days, depending on how deep into the desert you wish to venture. Overnight camel treks often include camping under the stars, providing a chance to experience the desert's serene nighttime atmosphere.

Hot Air Balloon Rides

For a unique perspective of Wadi Rum, consider a hot air balloon ride. As you ascend, you'll gain a panoramic view of the desert's sweeping sands and rugged mountains. Balloon rides are typically scheduled for early morning to take advantage of the calm winds and cooler temperatures. This experience allows you to see the intricate patterns and colors of the desert from above, creating a memorable highlight of your trip.

Rock Climbing and Hiking

Wadi Rum is also a haven for rock climbers and hikers. The area offers a variety of climbing routes and trails suitable for all levels of experience. The towering rock formations and steep cliffs present challenges for seasoned climbers, while easier hikes allow you to explore the desert's unique geological features and natural beauty. Notable climbing spots include **Jebel Rum** and **Jebel Umm Adaami**, the latter being Jordan's highest peak.

Practical Tips for Visiting Wadi Rum

When planning your visit to Wadi Rum, keep these tips in mind to ensure a smooth and enjoyable experience:

Timing Your Visit: The best time to visit Wadi Rum is during the cooler months from October to April. Summer temperatures can be extreme, often exceeding 40°C (104°F), which can make outdoor activities uncomfortable.

What to Wear: Dress in lightweight, breathable clothing and wear a hat to protect yourself from the sun. Sturdy shoes are essential for hiking and exploring the rocky terrain.

Stay Hydrated: The desert climate can be very dry, so it's important to drink plenty of water. Many tours will provide water, but it's a good idea to carry extra supplies.

Sun Protection: Use sunscreen, sunglasses, and lip balm with SPF to protect your skin from the harsh desert sun.

Respect Local Customs: When visiting Bedouin camps or interacting with the local people, be mindful of cultural norms and show respect for their traditions and ways of life.

Address and Location

Wadi Rum is located in southern Jordan, approximately 70 kilometers (43 miles) from the city of Aqaba. The desert is accessible by car, with various tour operators and Bedouin camps offering transport from Aqaba and Petra. The main entrance to Wadi Rum, where you'll need to obtain a permit to enter the protected area, is known as the **Wadi Rum Visitor Center**, located at GPS coordinates 29.5572° N, 35.4068° E.

Overnight Stays

If you choose to stay overnight in Wadi Rum, several Bedouin camps offer comfortable accommodations. These camps provide traditional meals, desert excursions, and opportunities to experience Bedouin culture up close. Reservations are recommended, especially during peak travel seasons.

Dead Sea

The Dead Sea, situated in the Jordan Rift Valley, is a unique and extraordinary destination renowned for its therapeutic properties and stunning natural beauty. This saltwater lake, lying at the Earth's lowest point on land, provides visitors with an unparalleled floating experience and offers a range of health benefits that attract travelers from around the world.

Floating Experience
The Dead Sea's high salinity—about 30%—creates a buoyant environment that allows you to float effortlessly on its surface. The lake's saline concentration is significantly higher than any other body of water, making floating a unique and enjoyable experience. When you visit the Dead Sea, you'll find that you can lie on your back and read a newspaper, all without the fear of sinking.

The high salt content, primarily sodium chloride, along with other minerals like magnesium, potassium, and calcium, contributes to this buoyancy. These minerals also provide the lake's distinctive and therapeutic properties. To maximize your floating experience, follow these steps:

Preparation: Before entering the water, ensure your skin is clean and free from any lotions or oils. These can affect the floating experience and might irritate your skin when in contact with the salt.

Entry: Gently wade into the water, starting from the shallow areas. The water temperature is typically warm and comfortable, ranging from 20°C to 37°C (68°F to 98°F), making it pleasant for a relaxing soak.

Floating Technique: Once in deeper water, lie back and let your body naturally float. Keep your legs slightly spread and your arms relaxed at your sides. Avoid splashing or vigorous movements, as they can disrupt the floating experience.

Duration: Limit your time in the water to around 15-20 minutes at a time to avoid skin irritation. The high salt concentration can cause dryness and irritation if you're exposed for too long.

Health Benefits
The Dead Sea's mineral-rich waters offer various health benefits, particularly for those with skin conditions and musculoskeletal issues. The following are some key benefits:

Skin Health: The minerals in the Dead Sea water, including magnesium, calcium, and potassium, are known to improve skin hydration, reduce inflammation, and enhance overall skin health. Regular soaking in these waters can help alleviate symptoms of skin conditions such as psoriasis, eczema, and acne. The mud from the Dead Sea is also renowned for its therapeutic properties and is used in various cosmetic treatments. Applying Dead Sea mud can help cleanse and rejuvenate your skin, leaving it softer and more supple.

Joint and Muscle Relief: The warm, mineral-rich waters provide relief from muscle tension and joint pain. Magnesium, in particular, is known for its muscle-relaxing properties and can help ease conditions like arthritis and fibromyalgia. The buoyancy of the water reduces the strain on joints and muscles, allowing for gentle exercise and movement without discomfort.

Detoxification: The Dead Sea's high salt content helps draw out toxins from the body. Immersing yourself in the mineral-rich waters can aid in detoxifying your skin and improving overall health. Additionally, the mud baths available at the Dead Sea resorts can further enhance the detoxification process.

Stress Reduction: Floating in the Dead Sea's warm, mineral-rich waters provides a calming and relaxing experience. The buoyancy of the water and the therapeutic properties of the minerals contribute to stress relief and mental relaxation. Many visitors find the experience to be a significant mood booster and a great way to unwind.

Visiting the Dead Sea
Several resorts and public beaches along the Jordanian side of the Dead Sea provide access to the waters and additional amenities. Some notable locations include:

Dead Sea Resort: Located at Sweimeh, the Dead Sea Resort offers private beach access and various spa treatments utilizing Dead Sea minerals. Address: Sweimeh, Dead Sea, Jordan. Opening hours vary, typically from 8:00 AM to 6:00 PM.

Kempinski Hotel Ishtar Dead Sea: This luxury hotel features an exclusive private beach, multiple swimming pools, and a comprehensive spa. Address: Dead Sea Road, Sweimeh, Jordan. The hotel's facilities are available to guests and non-residents, with opening hours for the spa and beach typically from 8:00 AM to 7:00 PM.

Amman Beach: A more budget-friendly option, Amman Beach offers public access to the Dead Sea with essential amenities. Address: Dead Sea Road, Amman, Jordan. The beach is usually open from 8:00 AM to 6:00 PM.

Important Considerations
Sun Protection: The Dead Sea area is known for its intense sunlight and high UV levels. Always apply sunscreen with high SPF before entering the water, and wear a wide-brimmed hat and protective clothing to avoid sunburn.

Hydration: The high salt content can lead to dehydration, so drink plenty of water before and after your visit to the Dead Sea. Avoid drinking the water from the lake, as it is highly saline and can be harmful if ingested.

Safety: While floating is a unique experience, avoid diving or splashing. The high salt content can irritate your eyes and mucous membranes. Rinse off with fresh water after exiting the Dead Sea to remove any residual salt from your skin.

Ajloun Forest Reserve

Location and Accessibility
The Ajloun Forest Reserve is located about 76 kilometers north of Amman, the capital of Jordan. It can be reached by taking the main highway from Amman towards Ajloun. The journey typically takes around an hour and a half by car. If you're using public transportation, you can take a bus from Amman to Ajloun and then arrange for a local taxi to the reserve. The address for the reserve is:

Ajloun Forest Reserve, Ajloun Governorate, Jordan
The reserve is open to visitors daily, with regular opening hours from 8:00 AM to 4:00 PM, though hours may vary seasonally, so it is advisable to check ahead.

Natural Beauty and Biodiversity
Ajloun Forest Reserve is renowned for its rich biodiversity, hosting a range of species that are representative of Jordan's natural habitats. The reserve is situated within the highland forests of the Ajloun Highlands, characterized by its dense oak, pistachio, and wild strawberry trees. This forest area forms part of the Mediterranean woodlands, providing a cooler, green refuge compared to the surrounding arid landscapes of Jordan.
In terms of wildlife, Ajloun is home to several notable species, including the Arabian red fox, the striped hyena, and the golden jackal. Birdwatchers will appreciate the opportunity to spot various bird species such as the Syrian woodpecker and the long-legged buzzard. The

reserve also supports a population of the rare and elusive wildcat, which adds to its allure for wildlife enthusiasts.

Activities and Trails

The Ajloun Forest Reserve offers a range of activities designed to help you immerse yourself in its natural beauty. One of the main attractions is the network of hiking trails that wind through the forest. These trails vary in difficulty, catering to both casual walkers and more experienced hikers. The trails offer opportunities to observe the reserve's diverse plant and animal life, with informative signposts providing insights into the local ecology.

The most popular trail is the **"Salamuni Trail,"** which spans about 2.5 kilometers and offers a moderate hike through some of the reserve's most picturesque areas. Along the way, you will encounter dense woodlands and open meadows, as well as stunning viewpoints overlooking the surrounding countryside. This trail is ideal for those who want to experience the reserve's natural splendor without committing to a more strenuous hike.

For a more challenging experience, consider the **"Jabal al-Hussein Trail,"** which extends for approximately 5 kilometers and includes steeper ascents and more rugged terrain. This trail provides a more comprehensive exploration of the reserve and rewards hikers with panoramic views of the Ajloun Hills and the distant Jordan Valley.

Visitor Center and Facilities

The reserve's visitor center is an excellent starting point for your trip. Located near the entrance, the center provides maps, information about the reserve's ecology, and details on available tours. Here, you can also find a small shop selling local handicrafts and souvenirs. The visitor center features exhibits on the flora and fauna of the reserve and offers educational programs and workshops, especially during weekends and school holidays.

Rest areas are available along the trails, allowing you to pause and enjoy a picnic amid the forest's tranquility. These spots are equipped with benches and tables, and there are designated areas for barbecuing if you wish to prepare your own meal.

Conservation Efforts and Sustainable Tourism

Ajloun Forest Reserve is managed by the Royal Society for the Conservation of Nature (RSCN), which plays a crucial role in the reserve's conservation efforts. The RSCN focuses on maintaining the ecological balance of the reserve, protecting endangered species, and promoting sustainable tourism practices.

As a visitor, you are encouraged to follow guidelines to minimize your impact on the environment. Stick to designated trails to avoid disturbing wildlife and trampling on delicate plant life. Dispose of waste responsibly by using the provided bins, and avoid picking plants or feeding animals.

Nearby Attractions

While visiting Ajloun Forest Reserve, you may also want to explore nearby attractions. The **Ajloun Castle,** located about 15 kilometers from the reserve, offers a fascinating glimpse into Jordan's medieval history. This 12th-century fortress provides panoramic views of the surrounding landscape and is an excellent complement to your visit to the reserve.

Another nearby site is the **Mujib Nature Reserve**, located approximately 60 kilometers south of Ajloun. This reserve is known for its dramatic landscape and offers opportunities for water-based adventures, including canyoning and river hiking.

Mujib Nature Reserve

Location and Access

The Mujib Nature Reserve is situated in the southwest of Jordan, bordering the Dead Sea. Its main entrance is located near the village of Mukhaybib, about 90 kilometers from Amman and 45 kilometers from the Dead Sea resorts. The reserve is easily accessible via the road leading to the Dead Sea, with clear signs directing visitors to the entrance. The reserve is open to visitors daily from 8:00 AM to 4:00 PM, with extended hours during the summer months.

The Siq Trail: An Adventure Through Time
One of the most popular attractions within the Mujib Nature Reserve is the Siq Trail, an adventure that takes you through a stunning canyon carved by ancient watercourses. The Siq Trail is a must-do for those looking to experience the reserve's natural wonders firsthand.

Trail Overview
The Siq Trail spans approximately 2.5 kilometers and takes around 2 to 3 hours to complete, depending on your pace and the time spent exploring. The trail follows a narrow canyon with high, sheer rock walls, creating a dramatic and picturesque environment. As you hike through the Siq, you'll traverse through shallow water, walk along rocky paths, and navigate natural obstacles, making for an adventurous and engaging experience.

What to Expect
The Siq Trail is characterized by its varied terrain. You will encounter sections where you need to wade through water, rock-scramble, and even climb small rock formations. The water level can vary depending on the season and recent rainfall, so it's important to check current conditions before setting out. The canyon's high walls and the serene flow of the stream create a unique atmosphere that enhances the sense of adventure.

Along the trail, you'll have the opportunity to witness the diverse flora and fauna of the reserve. Keep an eye out for various bird species, including the Sinai rosefinch and the Nubian ibex, which are native to the region. The reserve's flora includes hardy plants adapted to the arid environment, such as acacias and wild thyme.

What to Bring
To fully enjoy the Siq Trail, be sure to bring appropriate footwear, such as water-resistant hiking boots or sturdy sandals with good traction. Since parts of the trail involve wading through water, wearing quick-dry clothing and a swimsuit is advisable. Additionally, bring plenty of water to stay hydrated, sunscreen, and a hat to protect yourself from the sun.

Adventure Activities Beyond the Siq Trail

Aside from the Siq Trail, the Mujib Nature Reserve offers a variety of other adventure activities, catering to different interests and fitness levels.

Canyoning

Canyoning is one of the reserve's most thrilling activities. It involves descending through canyons by rappelling, climbing, and swimming. The reserve provides guided canyoning tours that include all necessary equipment and safety briefings. The most popular canyoning route in Mujib is the Wadi Mujib Canyon, which offers a combination of climbing, swimming, and rappelling. This activity is ideal for those seeking a high-adrenaline adventure amidst stunning natural scenery.

Bird Watching

Mujib Nature Reserve is also an excellent destination for bird watching. The reserve's varied habitats, from rocky canyons to lush vegetation along the watercourses, attract a diverse range of bird species. Early morning or late afternoon are the best times for bird watching, as many species are most active during these periods. Bring a pair of binoculars and a field guide to enhance your bird-watching experience.

Hiking and Nature Walks

In addition to the Siq Trail, the reserve offers several other hiking trails and nature walks. These trails vary in difficulty and length, providing options for all levels of hikers. Some trails take you through different ecosystems within the reserve, allowing you to experience the varied landscapes and wildlife.

Conservation and Visitor Information

The Mujib Nature Reserve is managed by the Royal Society for the Conservation of Nature (RSCN), which is committed to preserving the reserve's unique ecosystems and biodiversity. As a visitor, you play a crucial role in this effort by following the reserve's guidelines and respecting the natural environment.

Rules and Guidelines
Stay on Designated Trails: To minimize environmental impact, stick to marked trails and avoid disturbing wildlife.

Follow Safety Instructions: Adhere to safety guidelines provided by your guides or posted signs. This is particularly important for adventure activities like canyoning.

No Littering: Carry out all your trash and dispose of it properly to keep the reserve clean.

Respect Wildlife: Observe animals from a distance and do not feed or touch them.

Practical Tips for Visiting
Check Weather Conditions: Weather can impact trail conditions and water levels. Check forecasts and trail updates before visiting.

Prepare for Water Activities: If engaging in water-based activities, ensure you have waterproof gear and check the water levels.

Hire a Guide: For activities like canyoning, it's advisable to hire a local guide who knows the area and can ensure your safety.

Chapter 6:

Outdoor Activities and Adventures

Hiking and Trekking Trails

Wadi Rum

Wadi Rum, also known as the Valley of the Moon, is a vast desert wilderness that boasts stunning rock formations, sweeping sand dunes, and ancient petroglyphs. The area is a paradise for adventure enthusiasts and is famous for its dramatic landscapes.

Trail: The "Lawrence's Spring" trail is a popular choice, offering breathtaking views of the desert landscape and the opportunity to explore historical sites related to T.E. Lawrence, also known as Lawrence of Arabia. Another recommended hike is the "Burdah Rock Bridge" trail, leading to a natural rock arch with panoramic views of the surrounding desert.

Duration: Depending on the trail, hikes can range from 2 to 6 hours.

Difficulty: Moderate to challenging. Some trails require climbing and scrambling.

Location: Wadi Rum Protected Area, southern Jordan. You can access the area from the village of Rum. Guided tours and treks are available from local tour operators.

Opening Hours: Accessible year-round; guided tours generally run from sunrise to sunset.

Petra

Petra, the Rose City, is renowned for its ancient rock-cut architecture and historical significance. Hiking here allows you to explore hidden corners of this UNESCO World Heritage Site, offering both stunning views and historical insights.

Trail: The "Al-Khubtha Trail" is highly recommended, leading you to a vantage point offering panoramic views of Petra's rock formations and archaeological sites. Another intriguing route is the "Petra Monastery Trail," which climbs through rugged terrain to the impressive Monastery.

Duration: Trails can range from 2 to 5 hours.

Difficulty: Moderate. Expect some uphill sections and uneven terrain.

Location: Petra Archaeological Park, Ma'an Governorate, southern Jordan. The entrance is from the Petra Visitor Center.

Opening Hours: The park is open from 6:00 AM to 6:00 PM, with extended hours during peak season.

The Jordan Trail

The Jordan Trail is a long-distance hiking route stretching approximately 650 kilometers from the northern border with Syria to the southern tip at Aqaba. It traverses diverse landscapes, including deserts, mountains, and valleys.

Trail: The "Dana to Petra" section of the Jordan Trail is particularly notable, offering dramatic changes in scenery from the highlands of Dana Nature Reserve to the ancient ruins of Petra. This section passes through deep canyons, arid deserts, and lush valleys.

Duration: The entire trail can take up to 40 days to complete, but shorter sections can be hiked in 3 to 5 days.

Difficulty: Moderate to challenging, depending on the section.

Location: The Jordan Trail starts in Um Qais and ends in Aqaba, passing through various towns and nature reserves. Specific trailheads can be accessed from major cities like Amman and Petra.

Opening Hours: The trail is accessible year-round, though the best time to hike is from March to May and September to November.

Wadi Mujib

Wadi Mujib is known for its stunning river canyon and lush vegetation, contrasting sharply with the surrounding desert. It is one of Jordan's most accessible natural reserves, offering thrilling adventure opportunities.

Trail: The "Siq Trail" is the most famous and involves walking through the river, climbing rocks, and navigating narrow gorges. This trail provides a unique way to experience the canyon's beauty and is ideal for those seeking a water-based adventure.

Duration: The trail typically takes about 2 to 3 hours.

Difficulty: Moderate to challenging. Expect water and rock scrambling.

Location: Wadi Mujib Nature Reserve, located 90 kilometers south of Amman. The visitor center is at the entrance to the reserve.

Opening Hours: Open from 8:00 AM to 5:00 PM during the summer and 8:00 AM to 4:00 PM in winter.

Ajloun Forest Reserve

Ajloun Forest Reserve is a lush area with diverse flora and fauna, offering a contrast to Jordan's arid landscapes. The reserve is ideal for those interested in forested trails and wildlife.

Trail: The "Ajloun Nature Trail" winds through oak and pine forests, providing a peaceful hiking experience with opportunities for birdwatching. Another option is the "Wadi Bin Hammad Trail," which offers scenic views of the reserve's valleys and waterfalls.

Duration: Trails range from 1 to 3 hours.

Difficulty: Easy to moderate, suitable for casual hikers and families.

Location: Ajloun Governorate, northern Jordan. The reserve is accessible from the town of Ajloun.

Opening Hours: The reserve is open from 8:00 AM to 4:00 PM during the summer and 8:00 AM to 3:00 PM in winter.

Umm Qais

Umm Qais, an ancient Greco-Roman city, offers unique hiking opportunities combined with historical exploration. The site provides expansive views over the Golan Heights and the Sea of Galilee.

Trail: The "Umm Qais Archaeological Trail" takes you through the ruins of the ancient city and offers spectacular views of the surrounding landscape. This trail provides insight into the historical significance of the area while allowing you to enjoy the natural beauty.

Duration: About 2 hours.

Difficulty: Easy to moderate, suitable for all levels of hikers.

Location: Umm Qais, northern Jordan. The site is accessible from the town of Umm Qais.

Opening Hours: The site is open from 8:00 AM to 4:00 PM.

Scuba Diving and Snorkeling in Aqaba

Scuba Diving in Aqaba
Diving Sites and Coral Reefs

Aqaba's underwater environment is characterized by stunning coral reefs and marine ecosystems. The most famous sites include:

The Japanese Gardens: Located about 7 kilometers from the shore, this site is known for its diverse coral formations and abundant fish species. The gardens are characterized by intricate coral structures and clear waters, making it a favorite among divers.

The Cedar Pride Wreck: This sunken cargo ship lies at a depth of 28 meters and is one of Aqaba's most popular wreck dives. The vessel has become an artificial reef, teeming with marine life including lionfish, groupers, and moray eels. It's suitable for both advanced and beginner divers.

The Yamanieh Reef: Renowned for its pristine coral gardens and excellent visibility, Yamanieh Reef offers a unique underwater landscape. Divers can expect to see a variety of reef fish, including parrotfish and butterflyfish, as well as occasional sightings of larger pelagic species.

Diving Operators and Centers

Several dive operators in Aqaba offer guided dives, rental equipment, and certification courses. Prominent centers include:

Aqaba Marine Park Dive Center: Located within the Aqaba Marine Park, this center provides comprehensive dive packages, including guided dives, equipment rental, and certification courses. Address: South Beach Road, Aqaba. Opening hours: Daily from 8 AM to 6 PM.

Red Sea Dive Center: Known for its experienced instructors and personalized service, this center offers a range of diving experiences from beginner to advanced levels. Address: Al-Hussein Bin Abdullah Street, Aqaba. Opening hours: Daily from 8 AM to 7 PM.

Dive Aqaba: Specializing in both recreational and technical diving, Dive Aqaba provides high-quality equipment and professional guides. Address: King Hussein Street, Aqaba. Opening hours: Daily from 8 AM to 5 PM.

Safety and Regulations
Safety is paramount in scuba diving. Ensure you follow these guidelines:

Certification: Divers should hold a recognized certification, such as PADI or NAUI. For beginners, taking a certification course before diving is highly recommended.

Health: Ensure you are in good health before diving. Consult with a medical professional if you have any health concerns.

Equipment: Always use well-maintained equipment. Verify your gear before each dive, including your regulator, buoyancy control device, and wetsuit.

Environmental Protection: Avoid touching or disturbing marine life and refrain from collecting coral or shells. Follow the instructions of your dive guide to minimize impact on the environment.

Snorkeling in Aqaba
Snorkeling Spots
Aqaba's clear waters and rich marine life make it a prime location for snorkeling. Key spots include:

Coral Gardens: Situated close to the shore, Coral Gardens is an accessible snorkeling location where you can explore colorful corals and a variety of fish species. The shallow waters make it ideal for beginners and families.

Tala Bay: This resort area offers excellent snorkeling opportunities with easy access to coral reefs. The waters are calm, and the visibility is usually excellent, allowing you to see a wide range of marine life.

South Beach: Located near the dive centers, South Beach features a sandy bottom and coral patches. It's a popular spot for snorkeling, providing a chance to observe marine life in relatively shallow waters.

Snorkeling Operators and Equipment Rental

For those who do not have their own equipment, several operators offer snorkeling gear and guided tours:

Aqaba Adventure Divers: This operator provides snorkeling trips, including guided tours to the best spots in Aqaba. Equipment rental is available, and they offer snorkeling lessons for beginners. Address: North Beach Road, Aqaba. Opening hours: Daily from 8 AM to 6 PM.

Sea Star Water Sports: Located on the beachfront, Sea Star Water Sports offers snorkeling equipment rental and guided tours. Address: South Beach Road, Aqaba. Opening hours: Daily from 7 AM to 5 PM.

Aqaba Diving Center: Known for its professional service, this center provides high-quality snorkeling gear and guided snorkeling trips. Address: Al-Hussein Bin Abdullah Street, Aqaba. Opening hours: Daily from 8 AM to 6 PM.

Safety and Best Practices

To ensure a safe and enjoyable snorkeling experience:

Equipment: Use well-fitting masks and snorkels. Fins should be comfortable and appropriate for your level of experience.

Buddy System: Always snorkel with a buddy. This practice enhances safety and allows you to assist each other if needed.

Sun Protection: Wear sunscreen, a rash guard, or a wetsuit to protect your skin from sunburn. The sun can be intense, even in the water.

Marine Life Interaction: Avoid touching or feeding marine life. Maintaining a respectful distance helps protect both the animals and the ecosystem.

Environmental Considerations
Protecting Aqaba's marine environment is crucial. Follow these guidelines:
Avoid Touching: Refrain from touching corals or disturbing marine life. Even gentle contact can cause damage to sensitive coral reefs.

Waste Management: Dispose of waste properly. Littering in the ocean or on the beach can harm marine animals and ecosystems.

Responsible Photography: When taking underwater photos, ensure that your camera equipment is suitable for marine conditions and that you do not use flash, which can disturb marine life.

Jeep and Camel Safaris

Jeep Safaris
Overview
A jeep safari is an exhilarating way to explore Jordan's diverse terrain, from the rugged canyons of Wadi Rum to the serene desert expanses of the Black Desert. These off-road excursions are designed to take you deep into the heart of Jordan's most stunning landscapes, offering a combination of adventure and spectacular scenery.

Wadi Rum
One of the most popular destinations for jeep safaris is Wadi Rum, also known as the Valley of the Moon. This protected desert wilderness is renowned for its stunning sandstone mountains, vast open spaces, and unique rock formations.
Location: Wadi Rum, Jordan

Tour Operators: Numerous local operators offer jeep safaris, including Rum Stars, Wadi Rum Jeep Tours, and Bedouin Lifestyle. You can find these operators at the Wadi Rum Visitor Center.

Booking: It is advisable to book your safari in advance, especially during peak tourist seasons. Most tours can be arranged through your hotel or online through various tour operators' websites.

Duration: Safaris typically last between 4 to 8 hours, though full-day and multi-day options are available.

Experience

During your jeep safari in Wadi Rum, you'll traverse sandy plains, rocky outcrops, and ancient petroglyphs. Your guide will share insights into the area's geological history and the Bedouin way of life. Expect to see landmarks such as the Seven Pillars of Wisdom, a natural rock formation, and Lawrence's Spring, a historical site named after T.E. Lawrence.

Safety and Tips

Dress Code: Wear comfortable, breathable clothing and sturdy shoes suitable for rough terrain. A hat and sunglasses are essential to protect against the sun.

Health: Bring plenty of water to stay hydrated and use sunscreen to protect against sunburn.

Respect: Follow your guide's instructions to ensure safety and respect local customs, especially when visiting Bedouin communities.

Camel Safaris

Overview

Camel safaris offer a more traditional and leisurely way to explore Jordan's deserts. Riding a camel, or "ship of the desert," provides a unique perspective on the landscape and a glimpse into the age-old traditions of Bedouin nomads.

Wadi Rum

Camel safaris in Wadi Rum complement the jeep experience by allowing you to traverse more remote areas that are inaccessible by vehicle.

Location: Wadi Rum, Jordan

Tour Operators: Bedouin guides, such as those with Wadi Rum Bedouin Camp and Captain's Desert Camp, offer camel safaris. They can be arranged through the same local operators as jeep safaris or directly at the camps.

Booking: Reservations are recommended, particularly for longer treks. Book through local camps or online with reputable tour providers.

Duration: Camel safaris range from 1-hour rides to multi-day treks, depending on your interests and schedule.

Experience

On a camel safari, you'll ride through stunning desert landscapes, including sandy dunes and rocky formations. You'll likely pass by ancient rock carvings and might enjoy a traditional Bedouin meal under the stars. Camel rides offer a slower pace, allowing for a more contemplative experience of the desert environment.

Safety and Tips

Preparation: Camels can be tall, so be prepared for a bit of a climb when mounting. Your guide will assist you in getting on and off the camel safely.

Comfort: Wear loose, comfortable clothing and bring a light scarf to shield against the sun. Camel rides can be bumpy, so a cushion or padded seat might make the journey more comfortable.

Health: Hydrate well before and during your safari. The desert heat can be intense, so pace yourself and take breaks as needed.

Cultural Considerations

Both jeep and camel safaris in Jordan offer opportunities to interact with local Bedouins. The Bedouin people are known for their hospitality, and many tours include a visit to a traditional Bedouin camp where you can learn about their customs, enjoy traditional music, and taste local dishes.

Etiquette

Respect Local Customs: When visiting Bedouin camps or interacting with locals, dress modestly and seek permission before taking photographs.

Cultural Sensitivity: Bedouins value privacy and tradition, so approach with respect and courtesy.

Practical Information

Permits and Fees

Entrance Fees: Some areas, such as Wadi Rum, may require an entrance fee. Ensure you have sufficient local currency for these fees.

Permits: If you plan to venture into protected areas or nature reserves, check with your tour operator about any necessary permits.

Weather Considerations

Best Time to Visit: The best time for jeep and camel safaris is during the cooler months from October to April. Summer temperatures can be extremely high, making daytime activities challenging.

Climate: Be prepared for significant temperature fluctuations between day and night.

What to Bring

Essentials: Sunscreen, a hat, sunglasses, comfortable clothing, and sturdy shoes are essential. A camera, notebook, and binoculars might enhance your experience.

Rock Climbing and Canyoning in Jordan

Rock Climbing
Wadi Rum
Wadi Rum, also known as the Valley of the Moon, is a premier destination for rock climbing in Jordan. This desert region is renowned for its towering sandstone mountains, deep canyons, and natural arches. The area is home to numerous climbing routes, ranging from easy to advanced levels.

Climbing Areas: The most popular climbing areas in Wadi Rum include the Jebel Rum, Jebel Khash, and the Jebel Burdah. Each offers unique routes with stunning views and varying degrees of difficulty.

Guided Climbing: To ensure safety and maximize your climbing experience, consider hiring a local guide. Companies like **Wadi Rum Bedouin** (Wadi Rum, Jordan; +962 7 9527 8041) and **Rum Adventure** (Wadi Rum, Jordan; +962 7 9555 5286) offer guided climbing tours tailored to different skill levels.

Safety Considerations: Rock climbing in Wadi Rum requires proper equipment, including harnesses, helmets, and climbing shoes. Most climbing guides will provide these essentials, but it's best to confirm in advance. Ensure you are prepared for the desert environment by carrying sufficient water, sun protection, and appropriate clothing.

Ajloun Forest Reserve
For a different climbing experience, Ajloun Forest Reserve offers a cooler climate and lush landscape. This area features less challenging but equally scenic climbing routes compared to Wadi Rum.

Climbing Areas: The reserve has several routes on the rocky outcrops around the area. These routes are ideal for those who prefer climbing in a more forested environment.

Guided Climbing: Reach out to **Jordan Trail** (Ajloun, Jordan; +962 7 9080 8468) for climbing tours in Ajloun. They offer packages that include transportation and guiding services.

Canyoning
Wadi Mujib
Wadi Mujib is one of Jordan's most famous canyoning destinations. Known for its stunning canyons, waterfalls, and natural pools, this area provides a challenging yet rewarding adventure. The Mujib Biosphere Reserve offers several canyoning routes, each with its unique features.

Canyoning Routes: The most popular route is the **Siq Trail**, which involves wading through water, climbing, and rappelling. It's suitable for those with a moderate level of fitness and adventurous spirit.

Guided Tours: Mujib Adventure Center (Mujib Biosphere Reserve, Jordan; +962 7 9555 5188) provides guided canyoning tours, equipment rental, and safety briefings. They also offer different packages depending on the level of difficulty and duration of the adventure.

Safety Considerations: Canyoning in Wadi Mujib requires proper gear, including water shoes, wetsuits, and helmets. The Mujib Adventure Center supplies these, but it's crucial to check availability and size beforehand. Be prepared for water-based activities, so bring a change of clothes and waterproof bags for your belongings.

Wadi Dana
Wadi Dana, part of the Dana Biosphere Reserve, offers another excellent location for canyoning. This area is less crowded than Wadi Mujib and provides a more secluded experience.

Canyoning Routes: The **Wadi Dana Trail** is a popular route featuring scenic canyons, natural springs, and diverse wildlife. The trail includes sections of scrambling and water navigation.

Guided Tours: Contact **Dana Nature Reserve** (Dana Village, Jordan; +962 7 9527 1371) for information on canyoning tours in Wadi Dana. They offer guided experiences that include transportation and safety equipment.

Essential Tips for Both Activities
Permits and Regulations: Always check for any necessary permits or regulations before embarking on your adventure. Certain areas may require special permissions or have restrictions on climbing and canyoning activities.

Weather Conditions: Jordan's weather can vary significantly between regions and seasons. Check the weather forecast before your trip and be prepared for sudden changes. In desert areas like Wadi Rum, temperatures can soar, while higher altitudes in Ajloun and Dana may be cooler.

Health and Fitness: Ensure you are in good health and have a reasonable level of fitness before attempting rock climbing or canyoning. Both activities can be physically demanding and require a certain degree of stamina.

Respect the Environment: Jordan's natural landscapes are precious and often fragile. Follow the principles of "Leave No Trace" to minimize your impact on the environment. Stay on marked trails, avoid disturbing wildlife, and properly dispose of waste.

Wadi Rum Desert Adventures

Getting to Wadi Rum
Wadi Rum is located approximately 60 kilometers (37 miles) from the town of Aqaba and about 320 kilometers (200 miles) south of Amman. To reach the desert, you can either drive or arrange a transfer from Aqaba or Amman. The drive from Aqaba takes around 1.5 hours, while

from Amman, it takes approximately 4 hours. Be prepared for a scenic journey as you traverse the striking desert landscapes.

If you prefer not to drive, several tour operators offer guided transfers from major cities, providing convenience and expert knowledge. It is advisable to book your transport and activities in advance to ensure availability.

What to Expect

Wadi Rum's terrain is characterized by dramatic sandstone mountains, deep valleys, and vast expanses of desert. The area's natural beauty is complemented by its rich history, with archaeological sites and ancient petroglyphs that add cultural depth to your visit. The climate is arid, with hot days and cool nights, so pack accordingly.

Activities and Adventures

Jeep Safaris

One of the most popular ways to explore Wadi Rum is by taking a Jeep safari. These guided tours typically last between 4 to 8 hours and allow you to cover a lot of ground, experiencing the desert's diverse landscapes. You'll traverse sand dunes, rocky plateaus, and ancient rock formations. Most tours include stops at key sites such as Lawrence's Spring and the Khazali Canyon, where you can view petroglyphs left by early inhabitants.

Jeep safaris are ideal for those who want to see a lot in a short amount of time. Local guides are knowledgeable about the area's history and geology, providing valuable insights along the way.

Camel Treks

For a more traditional desert experience, consider embarking on a camel trek. Camel rides offer a slower, more immersive way to explore the desert. Treks can range from a few hours to several days, with options for overnight camping. During your ride, you'll get a unique perspective of the landscape and can enjoy the serene beauty of the desert at a relaxed pace.

Rock Climbing and Hiking

Wadi Rum is renowned for its excellent rock climbing opportunities. The area features numerous climbing routes suitable for all skill levels, from beginners to experienced climbers. The sandstone formations offer challenging climbs with breathtaking views. Ensure you have the necessary equipment and experience or hire a local guide who can provide safety gear and expertise.

Hiking is another great way to explore Wadi Rum's landscapes. Popular trails include the trek to Jebel Um Ishrin, known for its panoramic views, and the hike to the Burdah Rock Bridge, one of the desert's most iconic natural arches. Hiking in Wadi Rum allows you to appreciate the desert's natural beauty up close and at your own pace.

Hot Air Balloon Rides

For a truly unforgettable experience, consider taking a hot air balloon ride over Wadi Rum. These rides offer a bird's-eye view of the desert's stunning landscapes, providing a unique perspective on the area's vastness and beauty. Flights usually take place early in the morning or late in the afternoon to take advantage of the best light and weather conditions.

Stargazing

Wadi Rum's remote location and minimal light pollution make it an excellent spot for stargazing. The desert skies are incredibly clear, offering a spectacular view of the stars and planets.

Many campsites and tour operators offer stargazing experiences, where you can sit by a campfire and gaze up at the night sky, often with the guidance of an expert who can point out constellations and celestial objects.

Where to Stay

Wadi Rum offers a range of accommodation options, from luxury desert camps to budget-friendly options. Most accommodations are designed to blend seamlessly with the natural environment, providing a comfortable yet authentic desert experience.

Luxury Desert Camps

For a touch of luxury, consider staying at one of the high-end desert camps. These camps offer spacious tents with comfortable beds, private bathrooms, and sometimes even air conditioning. They provide gourmet meals and various amenities, including guided tours and cultural experiences. Popular luxury camps include the Sun City Camp and the Wadi Rum Luxury Camp, both offering exceptional service and stunning views.

Standard Desert Camps
Standard desert camps offer a more traditional experience with basic amenities. You'll stay in comfortable tents with shared bathrooms and communal dining areas. These camps often provide guided tours and cultural activities, giving you a chance to experience Bedouin hospitality. Camps like the Rahayeb Desert Camp and the Captain's Desert Camp are well-regarded for their hospitality and location.

Budget Options
For travelers on a budget, there are several affordable camping options available. These camps provide basic accommodations with shared facilities. Despite the simplicity, you'll still enjoy the stunning desert surroundings and the opportunity to experience Bedouin culture. Look for camps like the Bedouin Lifestyle Camp or the Wadi Rum Bedouin Camp for budget-friendly options.

Tips for Your Visit
Pack Appropriately: Bring lightweight, breathable clothing for daytime and warmer layers for cooler nights. Don't forget sunscreen, a hat, and sunglasses to protect yourself from the sun. Comfortable hiking boots are essential for exploring the desert's rugged terrain.

Stay Hydrated: The desert climate can be very dry, so drink plenty of water throughout the day to stay hydrated.

Respect Local Customs: Wadi Rum is home to the Bedouin people, who have their own customs and traditions. Be respectful of local practices and always ask for permission before taking photos of people or their property.

Book in Advance: Activities and accommodations can fill up quickly, especially during peak seasons. Book your tours and lodging well in advance to ensure availability.

Follow Safety Guidelines: Always follow the guidance of your tour guides and instructors, especially for activities like climbing and hiking. Safety is paramount in the desert environment.

Hot Springs and Natural Reserves

Hot Springs
Ma'in Hot Springs
Located about 64 kilometers south of Amman, the Ma'in Hot Springs offer a therapeutic escape from the hustle and bustle of city life. The hot springs are nestled in a picturesque valley, with mineral-rich waters cascading down the rocky cliffs. These natural hot springs are renowned for their healing properties, attributed to their high mineral content, including sulfur, calcium, and magnesium.
You can visit the Ma'in Hot Springs Resort, which provides several pools fed by the natural springs, offering a range of temperatures from warm to hot. The resort also features a spa where you can enjoy massages and other wellness treatments using the mineral-rich waters.
Address: Ma'in, Madaba Governorate, Jordan
Opening Hours: Daily from 9:00 AM to 6:00 PM

Hammamat Ma'in
A lesser-known but equally fascinating hot spring destination is Hammamat Ma'in. Located in the Ma'in region, these hot springs are less commercialized compared to their more famous counterparts. Here, you can experience a more natural and tranquil setting. The springs are

situated near the Dead Sea, providing stunning views of the surrounding landscape.

Address: Ma'in, Madaba Governorate, Jordan

Opening Hours: Daily from 8:00 AM to 5:00 PM

Dead Sea Hot Springs

The Dead Sea region, famous for its high salinity and therapeutic mud, also features natural hot springs. These springs are less prominent but offer an opportunity to combine the unique experience of floating in the Dead Sea with the soothing benefits of hot spring water. Several resorts around the Dead Sea, such as the Mövenpick Resort & Spa Dead Sea, provide access to these hot springs.

Address: Dead Sea Road, Sweimah, Jordan

Opening Hours: Varies by resort

Natural Reserves
Wadi Rum Protected Area

Known for its dramatic desert landscapes, Wadi Rum is a UNESCO World Heritage Site and a must-visit natural reserve in Jordan. The area is characterized by its vast sandstone mountains, deep valleys, and unique rock formations. Wadi Rum is also famous for its connection to T.E. Lawrence (Lawrence of Arabia), who explored this region during World War I.

In Wadi Rum, you can embark on various activities such as jeep tours, camel rides, and hot air balloon rides. The reserve offers several designated campgrounds where you can experience traditional Bedouin-style camping under the stars.

Address: Wadi Rum, Aqaba Governorate, Jordan

Opening Hours: Open year-round; specific tour times vary

Dana Biosphere Reserve

Dana Biosphere Reserve is Jordan's largest nature reserve, covering over 300 square kilometers. It encompasses a diverse range of ecosystems, from the semi-arid landscape of the desert to lush woodlands in the highlands. The reserve is home to various species of flora and fauna, including the Nubian ibex, the Syrian wolf, and numerous bird species.

The reserve offers a range of hiking trails, such as the Dana to Feynan Trail, which allows you to experience the stunning scenery and wildlife. The Dana Village, located at the entrance to the reserve, provides accommodation options and serves as a base for exploring the area.

Address: Dana, Tafila Governorate, Jordan
Opening Hours: Daily from 8:00 AM to 5:00 PM

Azraq Wetland Reserve

The Azraq Wetland Reserve, situated in the eastern desert of Jordan, is an important ecological site that supports a variety of bird species and other wildlife. The reserve features a series of interconnected wetlands, providing a crucial habitat for migratory birds such as the Great Cormorant and the Black-winged Stilt.

Visitors to the Azraq Wetland Reserve can explore walking trails and observation towers, which offer excellent opportunities for birdwatching and photography. The reserve also has a visitor center that provides information about the area's natural history and conservation efforts.

Address: Azraq, Zarqa Governorate, Jordan
Opening Hours: Daily from 8:00 AM to 4:00 PM

Mujib Nature Reserve

The Mujib Nature Reserve is situated near the Dead Sea and is known for its stunning canyons and rugged terrain. The reserve is named after the Mujib River, which flows through the area, creating dramatic landscapes and offering opportunities for adventure activities such as canyoneering and river trekking.

The Mujib Trail, also known as the Siq Trail, is a popular hiking route that takes you through narrow canyons and provides breathtaking views of the surrounding landscapes. The reserve's diverse habitats support a variety of wildlife, including the Nubian ibex and various bird species.

Address: Mujib, Madaba Governorate, Jordan
Opening Hours: Daily from 8:00 AM to 5:00 PM

Ajloun Forest Reserve

Located in the northern part of Jordan, Ajloun Forest Reserve is a lush green area that contrasts with the arid landscapes typically associated with the region. The reserve is characterized by its oak and pine forests, rolling hills, and scenic views of the surrounding countryside.

Ajloun Forest Reserve offers several hiking trails, such as the Saladin Trail, which allows you to explore the forest's diverse flora and fauna. The reserve also features a visitor center with exhibits on local wildlife and conservation efforts.

Address: Ajloun, Ajloun Governorate, Jordan
Opening Hours: Daily from 8:00 AM to 4:00 PM

Bird Watching in Azraq Wetland Reserve

The Azraq Wetland Reserve Overview

Address: Azraq, Jordan
Opening Hours: Daily from 8:00 AM to 4:00 PM, except Fridays and public holidays

Bird Watching Experience

The reserve's diverse habitats include open water, reeds, and surrounding semi-arid desert, creating a rich environment for various bird species. The wetlands are particularly renowned for their significance on the migratory routes of many birds.

Key Bird Species

Greater Flamingo: These striking pink birds are among the most iconic of the wetland reserve. Their presence is most prominent during the spring and autumn migration periods.

Eurasian Marsh Harrier: These raptors can often be seen gliding over the reed beds in search of prey.

Black-winged Stilt: Recognizable by their long legs and distinctive black-and-white plumage, they frequent the shallow waters of the reserve.

Crane Species: During migration seasons, several species of cranes, including the common crane, can be spotted as they rest or forage in the wetlands.

Best Times for Bird Watching

The best times to visit Azraq Wetland Reserve for bird watching are during the spring (March to May) and autumn (September to November). These seasons offer the most activity as many migratory birds pass through the reserve. Early morning is typically the best time to observe bird activity, as birds are more active in the cooler hours of the day.

Facilities and Services

The reserve is equipped with facilities to enhance your bird watching experience:

Visitor Center: The visitor center provides information about the reserve's ecology and bird species. It includes educational exhibits and offers guided tours led by knowledgeable staff.

Observation Towers: Strategically placed towers offer panoramic views of the wetlands, allowing you to observe birds without disturbing their natural habitat.

Nature Trails: The reserve features a network of trails for walking and guided tours. These trails are designed to minimize disturbance to wildlife while providing excellent vantage points for bird watching.

Rules and Guidelines

To ensure a respectful and enjoyable experience, adhere to the following guidelines:

Maintain Silence: Loud noises can disturb the birds. Keep noise to a minimum to avoid scaring away wildlife.

Stay on Designated Trails: Stick to marked paths to avoid disrupting the delicate habitats.

Avoid Feeding Birds: Feeding can alter their natural behaviors and diet. Let the birds forage naturally.

Respect the Wildlife: Do not attempt to touch or capture birds. Observe from a distance to avoid stressing them.

Additional Tips
Bring Binoculars and a Camera: High-quality binoculars and a camera with a zoom lens will significantly enhance your bird watching experience.

Wear Appropriate Clothing: The weather in the reserve can vary. Wear comfortable clothing and sturdy walking shoes, and be prepared for both sunny and cooler conditions.

Carry Water and Snacks: The reserve is large, and amenities are limited. Carry sufficient water and snacks to stay hydrated and energized.

Getting There
To reach Azraq Wetland Reserve from Amman, drive east on Route 40. The drive typically takes about one to one and a half hours. Signage along the route will guide you to the reserve's entrance. Public transportation options are limited, so consider renting a car or arranging a private tour.

Nearby Attractions
While visiting the reserve, you might also explore nearby attractions:

Azraq Castle: Located a short drive from the reserve, this historical castle offers insights into the region's history and panoramic views of the surrounding landscape.

Qasr al-Azraq: Another nearby site, this ancient Roman fortification provides a glimpse into the region's historical architecture and significance.

Conservation Efforts

The Azraq Wetland Reserve is part of Jordan's broader conservation efforts aimed at preserving the country's natural habitats. The reserve plays a crucial role in the survival of migratory birds and other wildlife. Supporting these conservation efforts by adhering to the reserve's guidelines and participating in educational programs helps protect this vital ecological resource.

Chapter 7:

Jordanian Cuisine and Dining

Traditional Jordanian Dishes and Cuisine

Mansaf

Mansaf is the crown jewel of Jordanian cuisine, often regarded as the national dish. It is a celebratory meal traditionally served during special occasions such as weddings, religious holidays, and family gatherings. Mansaf consists of lamb cooked in a fermented dried yogurt sauce known as jameed, served over a bed of rice and garnished with pine nuts and almonds. The dish is typically accompanied by a large, round, thin bread called shrak, which is used to scoop up the meat and rice. When dining on mansaf, you will experience the deep-rooted traditions and communal spirit of Jordanian culture.

Maqluba

Maqluba, meaning "upside-down" in Arabic, is a traditional Jordanian dish that offers a visual and culinary treat. It is a layered casserole of rice, meat (usually chicken or lamb), and vegetables such as cauliflower, potatoes, and eggplant. The dish is cooked in a pot and then carefully inverted onto a serving platter, revealing a beautifully layered and aromatic meal. Maqluba is a staple in Jordanian homes and is often enjoyed during family meals and gatherings.

Zarb

Zarb is a traditional Bedouin dish that showcases the ingenuity of desert cooking. It involves marinating lamb, chicken, or other meats with a blend of spices and herbs, then slow-cooking it in an underground pit oven. The meat is placed on a metal rack and covered with hot coals and sand, allowing it to cook slowly and absorb the smoky flavors. The result is tender, juicy meat with a unique taste. Zarb is often enjoyed in Wadi Rum, where Bedouin hospitality is at its finest.

Kunafa

Kunafa is a beloved Jordanian dessert that combines shredded phyllo dough with sweet, gooey cheese or cream, soaked in a fragrant syrup made from sugar, rose water, and orange blossom water. It is typically garnished with crushed pistachios and served warm. Kunafa is a staple at celebrations and special occasions, offering a perfect balance of sweetness and texture that will satisfy any dessert lover.

Falafel and Hummus

Falafel and hummus are iconic Middle Eastern dishes that are also central to Jordanian street food culture. Falafel consists of deep-fried balls made from ground chickpeas or fava beans, mixed with herbs and spices. They are often served in pita bread with fresh vegetables and tahini sauce. Hummus, a creamy dip made from blended chickpeas, tahini, lemon juice, and garlic, is a versatile accompaniment to many dishes. These two staples can be found at numerous street vendors and eateries across Jordan, providing a quick and delicious meal option.

Shawarma

Shawarma is a popular fast-food dish in Jordan and throughout the Middle East. It consists of thinly sliced marinated meat (usually lamb, chicken, or beef) that is stacked on a vertical rotisserie and slowly roasted. The meat is shaved off and served in pita bread or flatbread, along with vegetables, pickles, and sauces such as tahini or garlic sauce. Shawarma is a convenient and flavorful option for a quick bite while exploring Jordan's bustling cities and markets.

Mezze

Mezze is a traditional Jordanian appetizer spread that includes a variety of small dishes, allowing you to sample a range of flavors and textures. Common mezze items include:

Mutabbal: A smoky eggplant dip made with tahini, garlic, and lemon juice.

Tabbouleh: A fresh salad made from parsley, mint, tomatoes, onions, and bulgur wheat, dressed with olive oil and lemon juice.

Warak Enab: Grape leaves stuffed with rice, herbs, and sometimes minced meat.

Kibbeh: Deep-fried croquettes made from bulgur wheat and stuffed with spiced ground meat and pine nuts.

Labneh: Strained yogurt cheese, often drizzled with olive oil and served with bread.
Mezze is often enjoyed with friends and family, fostering a sense of community and sharing.

Mujadara
Mujadara is a simple yet satisfying dish made from lentils, rice, and caramelized onions. It is a staple in Jordanian households, offering a hearty and nutritious meal that is both flavorful and easy to prepare. Mujadara is typically served with yogurt or a side salad, making it a comforting and wholesome option for any time of the day.

Saj Bread
Saj bread, also known as markook, is a traditional Jordanian flatbread that is thin, soft, and slightly crispy. It is cooked on a convex metal griddle called a saj, giving it its distinct texture. Saj bread is versatile and can be used to scoop up dips, wrap around meat and vegetables, or simply enjoyed on its own. You can find saj bread being made fresh at local bakeries and markets, providing an authentic taste of Jordanian cuisine.

Dining Etiquette in Jordan

When dining in Jordan, there are a few etiquette tips to keep in mind to show respect for local customs:

Sharing is Caring: Jordanian meals are often served family-style, with large platters of food meant to be shared. It is customary to take small portions and leave enough for others to enjoy.

Use Your Right Hand: When eating with your hands, it is polite to use your right hand, as the left hand is considered unclean in Jordanian culture.

Compliment the Chef: Complimenting the host or chef is a way to show appreciation for their hospitality and the delicious food they have prepared.

Accepting Offers: If your host offers you more food or drink, it is polite to accept, even if you are already full. Refusing can be seen as impolite.

Pace Yourself: Jordanian meals can be lengthy affairs with multiple courses, so pace yourself and enjoy the variety of dishes without rushing.

Must-Try Street Foods

Shawarma

Shawarma is a staple of Jordanian street food and a must-try for anyone visiting. This popular dish consists of thinly sliced marinated meat, usually beef, lamb, or chicken, that is slow-cooked on a vertical rotisserie. The meat is typically seasoned with a blend of spices, including cumin, coriander, and paprika, giving it a rich flavor. Shawarma is usually served in a pita or flatbread with a variety of accompaniments such as tahini sauce, garlic sauce, pickles, and fresh vegetables.

You can find excellent shawarma throughout Jordan, but some notable spots include **Hashem Restaurant** in Amman. Located at **Al Hashemi**

St, Amman, Hashem is renowned for its shawarma, which is served with a side of traditional Jordanian pickles and freshly baked bread. They are open daily from **7:00 AM to 1:00 AM**, making it a convenient stop for any time of day.

Falafel
Another quintessential street food is falafel, which are deep-fried balls made from ground chickpeas or fava beans, mixed with herbs and spices. These crispy delights are usually served in pita bread with salad and tahini sauce. Falafel offers a savory, crunchy bite, complemented by the freshness of vegetables and the creaminess of the tahini.

Jafra Restaurant in Amman is a notable place to enjoy falafel. Situated at **Jabal Amman, 1st Circle, Amman**, Jafra has been serving delicious falafel for decades. The restaurant is open daily from **8:00 AM to 10:00 PM**, providing a reliable spot for falafel enthusiasts.

Mansaf
While not strictly street food, mansaf is a traditional Jordanian dish that you should not miss. It consists of lamb cooked in a sauce of fermented dried yogurt and served over rice with pine nuts and almonds. Mansaf is often enjoyed during special occasions and is considered the national dish of Jordan. Although it's usually served in restaurants rather than street stalls, trying mansaf is essential for a complete Jordanian culinary experience.

In Amman, **Sufra Restaurant**, located at **Jabal Amman, 1st Circle, Amman**, is an excellent place to try mansaf. The restaurant provides a traditional Jordanian dining experience with its extensive menu of local dishes. They are open daily from **11:00 AM to 11:00 PM**.

Kebabs
Kebabs are another popular street food item in Jordan. These skewers of marinated meat, often lamb or chicken, are grilled over an open flame, giving them a smoky flavor. Kebabs are typically served with a side of flatbread, salads, and dips. Street vendors across Jordan offer various types of kebabs, each with its unique blend of spices and marinades.

In **Downtown Amman**, you can visit **Al Quds Restaurant** located at **Al Hashimi St, Amman**. Known for its grilled kebabs, Al Quds provides a range of options from traditional kebabs to more adventurous choices. The restaurant operates from **8:00 AM to 10:00 PM** daily.

Hummus

Hummus, a creamy spread made from blended chickpeas, tahini, lemon juice, and garlic, is a fundamental part of Jordanian cuisine. While not exclusive to street food, hummus is often enjoyed as part of various street food dishes or as a standalone snack. It is commonly served with warm pita bread or as an accompaniment to kebabs and shawarma.

One of the best places to enjoy authentic hummus is **Abu Jbara** in Amman, located at **Rainbow St, Amman**. This establishment is well-known for its creamy hummus and other traditional dishes. They are open from **7:00 AM to 11:00 PM**.

Sfeeha

Sfeeha, also known as Arabic pizza, is a type of flatbread topped with minced meat, pine nuts, and a blend of spices. It's baked until the bread is crisp and the topping is flavorful and savory. Sfeeha can be found in bakeries and street food stalls throughout Jordan.

Al-Saraya Bakery, located at **Al Abdali, Amman**, is renowned for its sfeeha. The bakery is known for its fresh, delicious pastries and savory snacks. It is open from **6:00 AM to 9:00 PM** daily.

Mutabal

Mutabal, similar to baba ganoush, is a smoky eggplant dip mixed with tahini, garlic, and lemon juice. It is typically served with pita bread or as a side to other dishes. This dish provides a rich, velvety texture and a burst of flavor, making it a popular choice among street food lovers.

In **Amman**, **Fakhreldin Restaurant**, located at **Wadi Saqra, Amman**, offers excellent mutabal among other traditional dishes. The restaurant is open from **12:00 PM to 11:00 PM** daily.

Knafeh

For a sweet treat, try knafeh, a dessert made from layers of shredded phyllo dough, filled with a mixture of cheese or nuts and soaked in syrup. This indulgent pastry is often served warm and is a favorite among locals and visitors alike.

In **Jerash**, **Sweets of Jerash** at **Main Street, Jerash** is famous for its knafeh. This shop specializes in traditional Jordanian sweets and is open from **8:00 AM to 10:00 PM**.

Batata Harra

Batata Harra, or spicy fried potatoes, are seasoned with a mix of spices, garlic, and cilantro. This dish is a popular street food snack that offers a crispy exterior and a flavorful kick. It's commonly found in street food stalls and restaurants.

Al-Muheet Restaurant in **Amman**, located at **Al Weibdeh, Amman**, offers delicious batata harra. The restaurant is open from **11:00 AM to 10:00 PM** daily.

Tea and Coffee Culture

Tea Culture in Jordan

Tea in Jordan is more than just a drink; it's a social ritual. When visiting Jordan, you'll quickly notice that offering tea is a sign of hospitality and a gesture of goodwill. The most common type of tea served is black tea, often brewed strong and sweetened with plenty of sugar. It is typically served in small glasses, not cups, allowing the tea to cool quickly so you can enjoy it even in the heat.

Traditional Tea Houses

To fully appreciate Jordan's tea culture, consider visiting one of the traditional tea houses in Amman, such as **Tawaheen Al-Hawa**, located at Al-Wadi Saqra, Amman. Open daily from 10:00 AM to 11:00 PM, this tea house offers a genuine Jordanian tea experience. The tea here is often served with a side of traditional sweets like **Knafeh** or **Baklava**, making it a great place to immerse yourself in local flavors.

Another notable spot is **Al-Sultan Ibrahim**, situated in the heart of Madaba. This tea house is known for its serene ambiance and is open from 9:00 AM to 10:00 PM. It's an excellent place to enjoy a leisurely cup of tea while taking in the local atmosphere.

Mint Tea
Mint tea, or **Chai bil Na'na**, is a popular variation. It's usually prepared with fresh mint leaves and is especially refreshing in Jordan's hot climate. It's a traditional way to welcome guests and is often served during social gatherings or after meals. You might encounter mint tea in many local eateries and homes, where the fresh mint leaves are steeped along with black tea and sugar.

Coffee Culture in Jordan
Coffee holds a special place in Jordanian culture, with its own customs and rituals. The preparation and consumption of coffee are steeped in tradition. Jordanian coffee is typically prepared using finely ground Arabic coffee beans, which are roasted and brewed with cardamom. This blend gives the coffee a distinct aroma and taste.

Traditional Coffee Preparation
Jordanian coffee is usually served in small cups and is often accompanied by dates or other sweet treats. The process of making coffee is considered an art form and is done with great care. The coffee is brewed in a special pot called a **Dallah** and is traditionally poured by hand. If you're invited to a Jordanian home, accepting a cup of coffee is a sign of respect and friendship.

Notable Coffee Shops
For a genuine experience, visit **Café Hanin** in Amman, located at Shmeisani, which is open daily from 8:00 AM to 11:00 PM. This café combines traditional coffee-making techniques with a modern twist, offering a range of coffee options in a cozy setting. You can watch as skilled baristas prepare coffee using traditional methods.

Another excellent place is **Rumi Café** in Petra, located near the Petra Visitor Center. Open from 7:00 AM to 10:00 PM, this café provides a beautiful view of the ancient city while you enjoy your coffee. Rumi Café is known for its traditional coffee and the opportunity to experience the local coffee culture in a unique setting.

Coffee Rituals

Coffee rituals in Jordan often involve a process called **"Awh,"** where guests are served coffee in a specific manner. The host will pour the coffee from the dallah into a small cup and offer it to the guest. It's customary to take a sip and then return the cup to the host. Refusing coffee can be considered impolite, so if you're not inclined to drink it, it's best to accept the cup graciously and sip a small amount.

Dining Etiquette and Popular Restaurants

Dining Etiquette in Jordan

When dining in Jordan, adhering to local customs can greatly enrich your experience. Jordanian meals are often enjoyed with family and friends, and hospitality is a cornerstone of the dining culture. Here are some key points to keep in mind:

Respect for Tradition: Jordanians place great importance on hospitality. When invited to a local's home, it's customary to bring a small gift, such as sweets or fruits, as a gesture of appreciation.

Hand Washing: Before eating, wash your hands thoroughly, as Jordanian meals are typically eaten with the right hand. If you are offered food, you should accept it with your right hand only.

Eating with Your Hands: While utensils are available in most restaurants, traditional Jordanian dining often involves eating with your hands, especially for dishes like bread, dips, and grilled meats. Tear off a piece of flatbread and use it to scoop up dishes such as hummus, baba ghanoush, or grilled meats.

Sharing Meals: Meals are often served family-style, with several dishes placed in the center of the table for everyone to share. It's polite to try a bit of everything, and if you want more, ask for it directly.

Respect for Guests: If you are a guest in a Jordanian home, wait for the host to begin eating before starting your meal. It's also polite to finish everything on your plate, as leaving food may be seen as wasteful.

Dress Code: Dress modestly, particularly in rural areas or when visiting religious sites. This applies to both men and women, who should avoid wearing shorts or sleeveless tops.

Popular Restaurants in Jordan
Jordan boasts a variety of dining establishments ranging from traditional eateries to modern fine dining. Here are some must-visit restaurants that showcase the best of Jordanian cuisine:

Sufra Restaurant
Location: Jabal Amman, 3rd Circle, Amman
Address: 26, Omar Bin Al-Khattab Street, Jabal Amman
Opening Hours: Daily from 12:00 PM to 11:00 PM
Sufra Restaurant is renowned for its authentic Jordanian dishes and traditional ambiance. The restaurant is housed in a beautifully restored villa, offering a comfortable and elegant setting. Must-try dishes include mansaf (lamb cooked in a yogurt sauce), maklouba (a rice and vegetable dish), and a variety of mezze. Their fresh bread and rich desserts complete the dining experience.

Hashem Restaurant
Location: Downtown Amman
Address: 15, King Hussein Street, Downtown Amman
Opening Hours: Daily from 7:00 AM to 10:00 PM

Hashem Restaurant is a staple in Amman, famous for its simple yet delicious traditional dishes. Known for its falafel, hummus, and ful medames (stewed fava beans), Hashem offers a casual dining experience. It's a popular spot among locals and tourists alike, providing a taste of Jordanian street food in a welcoming environment.

Fakhreldin Restaurant
Location: Jabal Amman
Address: 3, Fakhreldin Street, Jabal Amman
Opening Hours: Daily from 12:00 PM to 11:00 PM
For a more upscale dining experience, Fakhreldin Restaurant is an excellent choice. It specializes in Lebanese and Jordanian cuisine, featuring a wide range of grilled meats, seafood, and vegetarian options. The elegant setting and attentive service make it a great venue for special occasions or a refined meal.

Wild Jordan Center
Location: Rainbow Street, Amman
Address: 13, Rainbow Street, Amman
Opening Hours: Daily from 10:00 AM to 10:00 PM
Located in the heart of Amman, Wild Jordan Center is an eco-friendly restaurant that promotes sustainable dining practices. It offers a variety of organic and locally sourced dishes, including fresh salads, sandwiches, and traditional Jordanian fare.
The center also provides stunning views of the city and is a great place to enjoy a meal while supporting local environmental initiatives.

The Jordanian Kitchen
Location: Petra
Address: Wadi Musa, Petra
Opening Hours: Daily from 12:00 PM to 10:00 PM
Near the iconic Petra archaeological site, The Jordanian Kitchen offers a relaxed dining atmosphere with a focus on local dishes. Enjoy a range of traditional Jordanian meals, including kebabs, shawarma, and flavorful rice dishes. The restaurant's proximity to Petra makes it a convenient stop for a hearty meal after a day of exploring.

Al Quds Restaurant
Location: Abdali
Address: 11, Abdali Boulevard, Amman
Opening Hours: Daily from 11:00 AM to 11:00 PM
Al Quds Restaurant is known for its diverse menu that combines Jordanian and Middle Eastern flavors. Popular dishes include grilled kebabs, biryani, and an array of mezze. The restaurant's contemporary setting and friendly service make it a popular choice for both locals and visitors.

Petra Kitchen
Location: Petra
Address: Wadi Musa, Petra
Opening Hours: Daily from 12:00 PM to 10:00 PM
Petra Kitchen offers a unique experience where you can participate in cooking classes and learn how to prepare traditional Jordanian dishes. The restaurant provides an interactive dining experience, allowing you to enjoy your own culinary creations in a welcoming environment.

Chapter 8:

Shopping and Souvenirs

Souvenir Shopping Tips

Local Markets and Souks

Amman: The capital city hosts several vibrant markets. The most famous is the Downtown Souk, located in the heart of the city. Here, you can find everything from traditional clothing to spices and handcrafted jewelry. For a more upscale experience, visit the Rainbow Street Market, open on Fridays, offering a mix of modern and traditional crafts.

Petra: Near the ancient city, the Petra Bazaar provides a range of items like Bedouin jewelry, woven textiles, and intricate pottery. Located just outside the main entrance to Petra, it is open daily from morning until the early evening.

Aqaba: This coastal city is known for its lively souks, particularly the Aqaba Souk, located near the city center. It's a great place to buy local handicrafts and sea-inspired souvenirs. The market typically operates from morning until late evening.

Haggling and Bargaining

Bargaining is a common practice in Jordanian markets. Start by offering about half of the seller's initial price and negotiate from there. Stay polite and friendly, as a good-natured negotiation can often lead to a better deal. Remember, the goal is to reach a fair price that both you and the seller are happy with.

Authentic Jordanian Souvenirs

Handmade Jewelry: Look for Bedouin silver jewelry, which often features intricate designs and semi-precious stones. These pieces are a beautiful reminder of Jordan's traditional craftsmanship.

Mosaics: Jordan is famous for its mosaic art, particularly from the Madaba region. You can find mosaic tables, coasters, and wall hangings. Visit the Madaba Mosaic School at Aisha Um al-Mu'mineen Street, Madaba, open from 8 AM to 4 PM, for authentic pieces.

Dead Sea Products: The minerals from the Dead Sea are known for their therapeutic properties. Products like mud masks, bath salts, and lotions are popular and widely available. Check out Rivage Dead Sea Cosmetics at Queen Rania Street, Amman, open daily from 9 AM to 7 PM.

Traditional Textiles: Items like keffiyehs (traditional scarves) and handwoven rugs make for excellent souvenirs. The Jordan River Foundation showroom at 40 King Abdullah II Street, Amman, is a reputable place to buy high-quality textiles, open from 10 AM to 6 PM.

Olive Wood Carvings: Skilled artisans carve beautiful figures and scenes from olive wood. These are commonly found in Christian pilgrimage sites like Madaba and Mount Nebo. For a wide selection, visit the Mount Nebo Handicraft Center, located on the road to Mount Nebo, open daily from 8 AM to 6 PM.

Supporting Local Artisans

Buying directly from local artisans not only ensures that you are getting authentic products but also supports the local economy. Look for cooperatives and foundations that promote fair trade practices. The Jordan River Foundation and the Al Balad Theatre Souk in Amman are excellent places to find genuine handmade products while supporting local communities.

Avoiding Fake Souvenirs

Be cautious of fake or mass-produced items, especially in tourist-heavy areas. Authentic Jordanian souvenirs typically have a unique, handcrafted quality. When in doubt, ask the vendor about the origin and maker of the item. Stores affiliated with the Jordan Tourism Board often have more reliable products.

Unique Shopping Experiences

Wadi Rum: In this desert region, you can find Bedouin-run stalls selling traditional goods. While exploring the stunning landscapes, take the opportunity to purchase unique items directly from Bedouin artisans. These stalls usually operate during daylight hours.

Ajloun Castle Market: Near the historic castle, there's a small market where you can buy locally produced honey, olive oil, and traditional handicrafts. The market is open daily from 8 AM to 6 PM.

The Souk Jara: Located on Rainbow Street in Amman, this seasonal market is open every Friday from May to September. It features a mix of local artists, food vendors, and crafters, providing a vibrant atmosphere perfect for finding unique souvenirs.

Payment and Currency

Cash is the preferred method of payment in most markets and souks. It's advisable to carry Jordanian dinars (JOD) in small denominations for easier transactions. While some larger shops might accept credit cards, it's best not to rely on them, especially in smaller towns and markets.

Cultural Etiquette

When shopping in Jordan, it's important to respect local customs. Dress modestly, especially in more conservative areas, and always ask for permission before taking photos of people or their stalls. Building a rapport with vendors can enhance your shopping experience and may even lead to better deals.

Transporting Souvenirs

Consider the size and weight of the items you purchase, especially if you're traveling by air. Mosaics, pottery, and other fragile items should be packed carefully to avoid damage. Many shops offer shipping services for larger items, which can be a convenient option.

Unique Souvenir Ideas
Arabic Calligraphy Art: Pieces featuring Arabic calligraphy make for beautiful and meaningful souvenirs. Visit galleries like Darat al Funun in Amman, located at 13 Nadeem al-Mallah Street, open from 10 AM to 7 PM.

Hand-painted Ceramics: Jordanian ceramics often feature traditional designs and vibrant colors. A recommended place to buy these is the Iraq Al-Amir Women's Cooperative, situated at Iraq Al-Amir, 15 km west of Amman, open from 9 AM to 5 PM.

Sand Art: Bottles filled with colored sand in intricate designs are a popular souvenir. You can find these in most tourist areas, but for a unique experience, visit the sand art shops in Wadi Rum, where you can watch the artists at work.

Handicrafts and Artisanal Products

Mosaic Art
Jordan is renowned for its intricate mosaic art, which dates back to ancient times. One of the best places to experience this is in the town of Madaba, often referred to as the "City of Mosaics." Here, you can visit the Madaba Archaeological Park, which showcases some of the most stunning examples of Byzantine-era mosaics.

Madaba Archaeological Park
Address: King Talal Street, Madaba, Jordan
Location: Central Madaba, near St. George's Church
Opening Times: 8 AM - 5 PM (Monday to Sunday)

For those interested in purchasing mosaic art, Madaba offers numerous workshops and galleries where artisans create and sell their works. These mosaics come in various forms, including wall hangings, tabletops, and decorative items, all showcasing intricate designs and vibrant colors.

Madaba Mosaic & Handicraft Center
Address: Al-Mouhafada Circle, Madaba, Jordan
Location: Near the Madaba Visitor Center
Opening Times: 9 AM - 6 PM (Monday to Saturday)

Bedouin Weaving
The Bedouin culture is an integral part of Jordan's identity, and their traditional weaving techniques are highly valued. Bedouin women weave rugs, blankets, and other textiles using natural dyes and traditional patterns that reflect their nomadic heritage. These items are not only functional but also serve as beautiful pieces of art.

Bani Hamida Women's Weaving Project
Address: Mukawir Village, Madaba Governorate, Jordan
Location: Near the historical site of Mukawir
Opening Times: 9 AM - 5 PM (Monday to Friday)
At the Bani Hamida Women's Weaving Project, you can purchase handwoven products directly from the artisans. This initiative supports local women and helps preserve their cultural traditions.

Ceramics and Pottery
The art of ceramics and pottery in Jordan can be traced back to ancient civilizations. Today, you can find beautifully crafted pottery items that are both functional and decorative. The town of Al Karak is known for its ceramic workshops, where skilled artisans produce a variety of items, including plates, bowls, vases, and tiles.

Al Karak Ceramics
Address: Al Karak, Jordan
Location: Near Al Karak Castle

Opening Times: 10 AM - 6 PM (Monday to Saturday)
These ceramics often feature traditional Jordanian motifs and patterns, making them perfect souvenirs to take home.

Dead Sea Products
Jordan is home to the world-famous Dead Sea, known for its mineral-rich waters and therapeutic properties. Dead Sea products, such as mud masks, bath salts, and skincare items, are highly sought after for their health benefits. You can find these products in various shops and spas throughout Jordan, but one of the best places to purchase them is at the source.

Dead Sea Spa Hotel Gift Shop
Address: Dead Sea Road, Sweimeh, Jordan
Location: At the Dead Sea Spa Hotel
Opening Times: 8 AM - 8 PM (Daily)
These products are made using natural ingredients from the Dead Sea and are perfect for pampering yourself or as gifts for loved ones.

Jewelry and Silverware
Jordanian jewelry, particularly silver jewelry, is renowned for its intricate designs and craftsmanship. Amman, the capital city, is home to numerous jewelry shops and markets where you can find beautiful pieces, including necklaces, bracelets, earrings, and rings. The designs often incorporate traditional Arabic motifs and are crafted using high-quality materials.

Amman Jewelry Center
Address: Rainbow Street, Amman, Jordan
Location: Near the First Circle
Opening Times: 10 AM - 9 PM (Monday to Saturday)
For a more traditional shopping experience, you can visit the souks (markets) in downtown Amman, where you can haggle for unique pieces.

Souk Jara

Address: Jabal Amman, Amman, Jordan
Location: Along Rainbow Street
Opening Times: 10 AM - 10 PM (Friday only, during summer months)

Olive Wood Products

The ancient olive trees of Jordan provide not only delicious olives and olive oil but also beautiful olive wood. Artisans craft a variety of items from olive wood, including kitchen utensils, decorative pieces, and religious artifacts. The town of Madaba is a good place to find these products, as many local workshops specialize in olive wood crafts.

Olive Wood Handicrafts Workshop

Address: King Hussein Street, Madaba, Jordan
Location: Near the Church of the Apostles
Opening Times: 9 AM - 6 PM (Monday to Saturday)
These items are known for their durability and the beautiful grain patterns of the wood.

Traditional Clothing

Traditional Jordanian clothing, such as the keffiyeh (headscarf) and thobes (embroidered dresses), are iconic symbols of Jordanian culture. You can find high-quality traditional clothing in various markets and shops across the country. The keffiyeh, typically in red and white or black and white, can be purchased in Amman's downtown markets.

Al Balad Souk

Address: King Faisal Street, Amman, Jordan
Location: Downtown Amman
Opening Times: 8 AM - 9 PM (Daily)
For embroidered dresses, the Souk Al-Sultan in the town of Salt is a great destination.

Souk Al-Sultan

Address: Al-Mutanabbi Street, Salt, Jordan
Location: Near the Great Mosque
Opening Times: 9 AM - 7 PM (Monday to Saturday)

These items make for meaningful souvenirs that represent Jordan's cultural heritage.

Spices and Herbal Products

Jordan's cuisine is rich in flavors, thanks in part to the variety of spices used in traditional dishes. You can take a piece of Jordanian culinary culture home by purchasing spices and herbal products from local markets. The Al-Husseini Mosque Market in Amman is a bustling spot where you can find a wide range of spices, herbs, and teas.

Al-Husseini Mosque Market

Address: King Talal Street, Amman, Jordan
Location: Near the Al-Husseini Mosque
Opening Times: 8 AM - 8 PM (Daily)
Commonly purchased spices include sumac, za'atar, and Jordanian seven-spice mix, all of which can add a taste of Jordan to your cooking.

Popular Markets and Bazaars

Amman – Souk Jara

Located in the heart of Amman's historic Jabal Amman district, Souk Jara is a vibrant outdoor market that operates every Friday from May to September. This bazaar is a hotspot for unique crafts, antiques, handmade jewelry, traditional garments, and local art. Walking through the market, you'll hear the sounds of traditional music and smell the aromas of Jordanian street food. It's a great place to buy souvenirs and mingle with locals and expatriates alike. The market opens from 10 AM to 10 PM, and it's situated along Rainbow Street, a popular tourist area.

Amman – Downtown Souk

Amman's Downtown Souk, located in the city center, is a bustling market where you can find a variety of goods, including spices, textiles, household items, and fresh produce. The market is divided into sections, each specializing in different products. The spice market, for instance, offers a colorful array of spices and herbs that are integral to Jordanian cuisine. Nearby, the gold market showcases intricately designed jewelry. This souk provides an authentic Middle Eastern shopping experience. The market is open daily from early morning until late evening.

Madaba – Madaba Artisan Street
Madaba, known for its ancient mosaics, hosts Madaba Artisan Street, a market dedicated to local crafts. Here, you can find beautiful mosaic artworks, traditional pottery, and other handicrafts made by local artisans. The market is a great place to buy unique souvenirs that reflect the rich cultural heritage of Jordan. The artisans often demonstrate their craft, providing insight into the traditional methods used. Madaba Artisan Street is open daily from 9 AM to 7 PM and is located near the St. George's Church, famous for its mosaic map of the Holy Land.

Aqaba – Aqaba City Center Market
Aqaba's City Center Market, located near the waterfront, offers a mix of traditional and modern shopping experiences. This market is perfect for buying souvenirs, local spices, and handicrafts. The market also has stalls selling fresh fish and seafood, reflecting Aqaba's coastal culture. The vibrant atmosphere, combined with the sea breeze, makes shopping here a pleasant experience. The market operates daily from morning until late evening.

Petra – Petra Souvenirs Market
Situated near the entrance of the ancient city of Petra, the Petra Souvenirs Market offers a variety of items perfect for tourists. Here, you can purchase traditional Bedouin jewelry, handmade pottery, and textiles. Many of the items sold here are made by local Bedouins, ensuring that your purchase supports the local community. The market is a great place to buy keepsakes that remind you of your visit to this iconic archaeological site. The Petra Souvenirs Market is open daily from 8 AM to 6 PM.

Irbid – Irbid Souk

Irbid's Souk, located in the city center, is a vibrant market where you can experience the northern Jordanian way of life. This market offers a variety of goods, from fresh produce to traditional garments and household items. It's a great place to buy local fruits and vegetables, as well as traditional Jordanian sweets. The friendly vendors are always willing to share stories and offer samples of their products. The market is open daily from early morning until late evening.

Salt – As-Salt Souk
As-Salt Souk, in the historic town of Salt, offers a glimpse into Jordan's past. This market, located in the town center, sells traditional goods such as spices, handmade soaps, and embroidered clothing. The souk's narrow streets and old buildings create a charming atmosphere. Shopping here feels like stepping back in time, with vendors offering goods that reflect the town's rich history. The market is open daily from morning until late afternoon.

Jerash – Jerash Handicraft Market
Near the famous Roman ruins of Jerash, the Jerash Handicraft Market offers a selection of locally made crafts and souvenirs. This market is an excellent place to buy traditional Jordanian pottery, embroidered items, and mosaic art. The vendors are often the artisans themselves, and they are happy to share the stories behind their work. The market operates daily from 9 AM to 5 PM and is located close to the main entrance of the archaeological site.

Wadi Rum – Bedouin Camps
While not a traditional market, the Bedouin camps in Wadi Rum offer a unique shopping experience. Bedouin families sell handmade jewelry, woven rugs, and other crafts directly from their tents. Purchasing items here supports the local Bedouin community and allows you to take home a piece of their rich cultural heritage. These camps are scattered throughout Wadi Rum, and shopping here is often part of the broader experience of staying in the desert.

Ma'an – Ma'an Market

Ma'an, a town in southern Jordan, hosts a traditional market where you can buy local produce, spices, and crafts. The market is a lively place, with vendors calling out to passersby and haggling over prices. It's an excellent place to experience the local culture and buy authentic Jordanian goods. The market is open daily from early morning until late evening.

Zarqa – Zarqa Souk
Zarqa Souk, located in the heart of Zarqa, is a bustling market offering a wide range of goods, from clothing to household items. This market is known for its affordable prices and diverse selection. It's a great place to shop if you're looking for bargains and unique items. The market is open daily from morning until late evening, and it's situated in the city center.

Bargaining Tips and Cultural Insights

Bargaining Tips
Bargaining is a common practice in Jordan, particularly in markets and souks. Here are some tips to help you navigate the bargaining process:

Start Low: When you're interested in an item, it's customary to start your offer at about half the asking price. This sets the stage for negotiation and indicates that you understand the bargaining culture.

Be Polite and Respectful: Always approach bargaining with a friendly and respectful attitude. Smiling and engaging in small talk can help create a positive interaction. Remember, bargaining is as much about the experience as it is about the price.

Know the Value: Before you start bargaining, try to get an idea of the item's value. This can be done by comparing prices at different stalls or asking locals for advice. Having a rough idea of what you should pay will give you confidence during negotiations.

Show Interest but Not Desperation: Express your interest in the item, but avoid showing that you must have it. This will prevent the seller from taking advantage of your eagerness and will help you negotiate a better price.

Be Prepared to Walk Away: One of the most effective bargaining tactics is being ready to walk away if the price isn't right. Often, the seller will call you back with a better offer.

Cash is King: Carrying cash is essential, as it is often preferred over credit cards, especially in smaller shops and markets. Having smaller bills can also make transactions smoother and help in negotiating a final price.

Cultural Insights
Understanding the local culture can significantly enhance your shopping experience in Jordan. Here are some cultural insights to keep in mind:

Respect for Tradition: Jordanians take great pride in their traditions and heritage. When shopping for traditional items such as Bedouin jewelry, handwoven rugs, or pottery, showing appreciation for the craftsmanship can create a more meaningful interaction.

Tea and Hospitality: It's not uncommon for shopkeepers to offer tea or coffee as a gesture of hospitality. Accepting this offer can be a great way to build rapport and may even lead to better bargains.

Language: While many Jordanians speak English, learning a few basic Arabic phrases can go a long way. Simple greetings like "Marhaba" (hello) or "Shukran" (thank you) can make a positive impression.

Dress Modestly: Modest clothing is appreciated, especially in traditional markets. Dressing conservatively shows respect for the local culture and can make your shopping experience more comfortable.

Time and Patience: Bargaining and shopping in Jordan are not rushed activities. Taking your time to browse, chat, and negotiate is part of the cultural experience. Patience is key to enjoying the process.

Popular Shopping Destinations
Souk Jara
Location: Rainbow Street, Amman
Opening Times: Fridays, 10 AM - 10 PM (May to September)
Souk Jara is a vibrant open-air market located in the heart of Amman. Here, you'll find a variety of stalls selling handmade crafts, jewelry, clothing, and artwork. It's a great place to pick up unique souvenirs and gifts. The market also features live music and food stalls, making it a lively spot to spend an afternoon.

Downtown Amman (Al-Balad)
Location: King Faisal Street, Amman
Opening Times: Daily, 9 AM - 9 PM
The downtown area of Amman, known as Al-Balad, is a bustling shopping district with a mix of traditional and modern stores. Here, you can explore the famous Gold Souk, where you'll find intricately designed jewelry. The Spice Souk is another highlight, offering a sensory experience with its array of aromatic spices and herbs.

Don't forget to visit the various shops selling traditional Jordanian attire, such as the keffiyeh (headscarf) and embroidered dresses.

Wadi Rum Visitor Center
Location: Wadi Rum Protected Area
Opening Times: Daily, 8 AM - 6 PM
In the stunning desert landscape of Wadi Rum, the visitor center features shops selling Bedouin crafts and souvenirs. You can purchase beautifully woven rugs, traditional Bedouin jewelry, and other handicrafts that reflect the heritage of the Bedouin people. These items not only make great souvenirs but also support the local communities.

Petra Visitor Center

Location: Petra, Wadi Musa
Opening Times: Daily, 6 AM - 6 PM
The Petra Visitor Center offers a variety of shops where you can buy authentic Nabatean artifacts, replicas, and locally made crafts. Items such as hand-carved stone figurines, pottery, and traditional Bedouin attire are popular choices. These souvenirs serve as memorable keepsakes from one of Jordan's most iconic sites.

The Jordan River Foundation Showroom
Location: 26 Al-Shareef Hussein Bin Ali Street, Amman
Opening Times: Saturday - Thursday, 9 AM - 5 PM
This showroom is part of the Jordan River Foundation, a non-profit organization dedicated to empowering local communities. Here, you can find beautifully crafted items made by local artisans, including home decor, textiles, and jewelry. Purchasing from this showroom not only provides you with high-quality souvenirs but also supports a worthy cause.

Must-Buy Souvenirs
Dead Sea Products: Known for their therapeutic properties, Dead Sea products such as mud masks, salts, and creams make excellent gifts. You can find these products at various shops across Jordan, including the Dead Sea region itself.

Olive Wood Carvings: Handcrafted olive wood items, ranging from kitchen utensils to religious artifacts, are popular souvenirs. These are available in many markets and souvenir shops.

Jordanian Spices and Herbs: The spice markets in Jordan are a feast for the senses. Look for unique blends such as za'atar (a mix of thyme, sesame seeds, and sumac) and sumac (a tangy spice made from dried berries).

Traditional Jewelry: Bedouin jewelry, often made from silver and adorned with semi-precious stones, is a beautiful keepsake. Each piece typically has a unique design that reflects Bedouin traditions.

Handwoven Rugs and Textiles: Jordanian rugs and textiles are known for their vibrant colors and intricate patterns. These items are often handmade by local artisans, making each piece unique.

Shopping Etiquette

Ask Before Taking Photos: While it's tempting to take pictures of the colorful markets and shops, always ask for permission before photographing people or their merchandise.

Respect Opening Times: Be aware of the opening and closing times of shops, especially in markets where vendors might take breaks during prayer times.

Tipping: Tipping is not mandatory but is appreciated, especially if you receive exceptional service or a particularly good deal.

Be Patient: Shopping in Jordan can be an immersive experience, so take your time to enjoy the sights, sounds, and interactions. Patience and a positive attitude will go a long way in making your shopping experience enjoyable.

Chapter 9:

Local Culture and Etiquette

Greetings and Social Customs

Traditional Greetings

In Jordan, greetings are an essential part of social interactions. When meeting someone, you will notice that Jordanians often use a warm and friendly approach. A common greeting is "As-salamu alaykum," meaning "Peace be upon you," to which you should respond with "Wa alaykum as-salam," meaning "And peace be upon you too." This exchange is a courteous way to show respect and establish a friendly tone.

Handshakes are common, particularly among men. When shaking hands, do so with your right hand, as the left hand is considered impolite for such interactions. Jordanians often place their left hand on their chest while shaking hands, which signifies sincerity and respect. If the handshake is particularly warm, it might be accompanied by a slight hug or kiss on both cheeks, starting with the right cheek.

Addressing People

When addressing Jordanians, it's customary to use titles and their first name. For example, "Mr. Ali" or "Mrs. Fatima." If the person holds a professional title such as "Doctor" or "Professor," it's respectful to use that title in your greeting.

Hospitality and Social Visits

Hospitality is a cornerstone of Jordanian culture. If you are invited to a Jordanian home, consider it an honor. It's polite to bring a small gift, such as sweets, fruit, or a souvenir from your home country. When entering a Jordanian home, you should remove your shoes unless instructed otherwise by your host.

During your visit, you will likely be offered tea or coffee. Accepting this offer is a sign of respect and appreciation. When served Arabic coffee, it's important to remember that it's traditionally served in small cups without handles. You should hold the cup with your right hand and accept at least one cup. Shaking the cup gently from side to side indicates that you do not want a refill.

Dining Etiquette

Mealtimes are important social occasions in Jordan. If you're dining at someone's home or in a traditional restaurant, there are a few key customs to keep in mind. Begin by washing your hands before the meal, as cleanliness is highly valued. Meals are often served on a communal platter, and you should use your right hand to eat. It's polite to try a little bit of everything offered to you, as refusing food can be seen as impolite. When the meal is finished, it's customary to thank your host by saying "Sahtein," which means "double health" and is akin to saying "bon appétit" after a meal.

Dress Code

While Jordan is relatively liberal compared to some of its neighboring countries, it's important to dress modestly, especially when visiting religious sites or rural areas. For men, long trousers and shirts with sleeves are appropriate. Women should wear clothing that covers their shoulders, upper arms, and legs. In urban areas like Amman, you'll find a more relaxed approach to dress codes, but it's still advisable to dress conservatively.

Religious Etiquette

Islam is the predominant religion in Jordan, and respect for Islamic customs is essential. When visiting mosques, you should dress modestly and remove your shoes before entering. Women are usually required to cover their hair with a scarf. It's also important to avoid visiting during prayer times unless you're there to participate.

Public Behavior
Public displays of affection are generally frowned upon in Jordan. It's best to avoid overt displays of affection such as kissing or hugging in public places. Holding hands is generally acceptable for married couples but might be less common in rural areas.

Respecting Personal Space
Jordanians value personal space and it's important to be mindful of this in social settings. When conversing, a respectful distance should be maintained, especially with members of the opposite sex. Physical contact beyond a handshake is generally reserved for close friends and family.

Photography
While Jordan's stunning landscapes and historical sites are perfect for photography, it's important to be respectful when taking photos of people. Always ask for permission before photographing individuals, particularly women, and be mindful of local sensitivities. Some religious sites may have restrictions on photography, so it's best to check beforehand.

Business Etiquette
In a business context, punctuality is valued, but meetings might not always start on time due to the flexible nature of social interactions. Business cards are exchanged after the initial greeting. It's courteous to spend a moment reading the card before putting it away. Business discussions often begin with small talk to establish a personal connection before moving on to the main topics.

Language and Communication
Arabic is the official language of Jordan, but English is widely spoken, especially in urban areas and among the business community. Learning a few basic Arabic phrases can go a long way in showing respect and building rapport. Jordanians appreciate any effort to speak their language, even if it's just simple greetings and expressions of thanks.

When communicating, be aware that Jordanians may use indirect language to avoid confrontation or giving a negative response. Reading between the lines and paying attention to non-verbal cues is important. Patience and politeness are highly valued in conversations.

Public Transport Etiquette
If you use public transportation in Jordan, such as buses or taxis, be aware of the local norms. It's customary to greet the driver and thank them when you exit. In shared taxis, men and women typically sit separately unless they are family members. Offering your seat to elderly passengers or women is a sign of respect and good manners.

Greetings and Social Customs

Understanding the Basics of Jordanian Etiquette
When visiting Jordan, it's crucial to understand and respect the local culture and social customs to ensure a pleasant and respectful experience. Jordanians are known for their hospitality and warmth, but there are specific norms and practices that every visitor should be aware of to avoid unintentional disrespect.

Greetings and Introductions
Greetings in Jordan are a significant aspect of social interactions. When meeting someone for the first time, a warm, genuine smile and a handshake are customary. For men, a firm handshake is standard, often accompanied by the Arabic greeting, "As-salamu alaykum," which means "Peace be upon you." The appropriate response is "Wa alaykumu as-salam," meaning "And peace be upon you too."
When greeting women, it's essential to be more cautious. If you are a man, wait to see if a woman extends her hand first. If she doesn't, a respectful nod or a slight bow is appropriate. For women greeting other women, a handshake is customary, and in more familiar settings, it's common to exchange cheek kisses, usually three times, alternating cheeks, starting with the right.

Respect for Elders and Hierarchy

Respect for elders and people in positions of authority is deeply ingrained in Jordanian culture. When greeting an elder, it is polite to stand up, use formal titles, and express respect verbally. Younger people often wait for elders to initiate greetings and may also kiss the forehead or hand of an elder as a sign of deep respect.

Social Customs and Hospitality

Hospitality is a cornerstone of Jordanian culture. When invited to a Jordanian home, it's customary to bring a small gift, such as sweets or flowers. Upon entering the home, you should remove your shoes. Expect to be offered coffee or tea as a sign of hospitality, and it is polite to accept. Declining multiple times is seen as rude, even if you are not particularly thirsty.

Jordanians are also known for their generous invitations to share meals. If you are invited to a meal, be prepared to eat heartily and compliment the food. It's considered impolite to leave food on your plate, as it may suggest that you did not enjoy the meal. Additionally, it's respectful to wait for the host to start eating before you begin.

Dress Code and Modesty

Modesty in dress is highly valued in Jordan. While urban areas like Amman might be more relaxed, it's advisable to dress conservatively, especially in rural areas. Men should avoid wearing shorts and sleeveless tops, while women should opt for clothing that covers their arms, legs, and chest. Headscarves are not mandatory for non-Muslim women, but wearing one in religious sites is a sign of respect.

When visiting religious sites, such as mosques, it is mandatory to remove your shoes before entering. Women should cover their hair, and both men and women should wear loose-fitting clothes that cover their arms and legs. It's also important to avoid loud conversations and to maintain a respectful demeanor while inside these sacred places.

Public Behavior and Interactions

Public displays of affection are frowned upon in Jordan. Holding hands and brief embraces are generally acceptable for couples, but anything more intimate should be reserved for private settings. Interactions between men and women should be conducted with a level of formality, especially in conservative areas.

It's also important to note that Jordanians place a high value on personal honor and reputation. Public criticism or arguments should be avoided as they can cause embarrassment and loss of face. If you have a disagreement, it's best to handle it privately and with tact.

Dining Etiquette

When dining in Jordan, there are a few customs to be aware of to show respect and courtesy. Meals are often communal, and food is typically shared from a large central platter. It's common to eat with your right hand, as the left hand is considered impolite for eating or passing food. If cutlery is used, it's generally for serving rather than individual use.

Before and after meals, it's customary to wash your hands. Some homes may provide a wash basin and water pitcher for this purpose. When offered food, it's polite to at least taste a small amount, even if you are not particularly hungry, to show appreciation for the host's efforts.

Gift Giving and Receiving

Gift-giving is a common practice in Jordan and is a way to show respect and appreciation. When giving gifts, avoid overly extravagant items, as modesty is valued. Suitable gifts include sweets, chocolates, or items from your home country. When receiving a gift, it's polite to accept it with both hands and express gratitude.

If you are invited to a wedding or another significant celebration, it is customary to bring a gift. Money is often given at weddings, presented in an envelope. The amount can vary depending on your relationship with the hosts, but it's always a good idea to be generous within your means.

Respect for Religion

Islam is the predominant religion in Jordan, and it significantly influences daily life and social customs. During the holy month of Ramadan, for instance, Muslims fast from dawn until sunset. As a visitor, it's respectful to avoid eating, drinking, or smoking in public during daylight hours. Many restaurants will be closed or offer limited services during the day, but they will open after sunset for Iftar, the meal that breaks the fast.

In general, avoid discussing sensitive topics related to religion or politics unless you are certain it will be well received. Jordanians are proud of their country and culture, and engaging in respectful, open-minded conversations can lead to meaningful connections.

General Politeness and Taboos

Jordanians value politeness and courteous behavior. When interacting with locals, using polite language and showing respect is essential. Avoid pointing at people, as it can be considered rude. Instead, use your whole hand to gesture.

Additionally, be mindful of body language. Sitting with the soles of your feet facing someone is considered disrespectful, as the feet are regarded as the lowest and dirtiest part of the body. When sitting, try to keep your feet flat on the ground or crossed at the ankles.

Dress Code and Modesty

General Guidelines

In Jordan, modesty in dress is highly valued, and it's important to dress conservatively to show respect for local customs and religious practices. Both men and women should avoid wearing revealing or tight-fitting clothing. While urban areas like Amman may be more lenient, rural and more traditional areas expect higher adherence to modesty.

Women's Attire

Women should aim to cover their shoulders, arms, and knees. Long skirts or trousers and blouses with sleeves are appropriate choices. Wearing a headscarf is not mandatory for non-Muslim women, but in some religious sites, covering your hair may be required. It's advisable to carry a scarf with you in case you need to cover your head when visiting mosques or other sacred places.

Men's Attire

Men should avoid wearing shorts, especially when visiting rural areas or religious sites. Long trousers and shirts with sleeves are considered respectful. Although short-sleeved shirts are generally acceptable, sleeveless tops should be avoided.

Religious Sites

When visiting religious sites such as mosques, it is crucial to adhere to specific dress codes. Women should cover their heads, arms, and legs, while men should wear long trousers and avoid sleeveless shirts. Shoes must be removed before entering a mosque, so wearing socks is advisable. Some notable religious sites include:

King Abdullah I Mosque: Located in Amman, this mosque is known for its stunning blue dome and is open to non-Muslim visitors. Women are provided with a robe to cover themselves before entering.

Al-Maghtas (Baptism Site): Situated near the Jordan River, this UNESCO World Heritage site is significant in Christian tradition. Modest clothing is required, and women should consider wearing a headscarf.

Urban vs. Rural Areas

In urban areas like Amman, you will find a more relaxed approach to dress codes, especially in places frequented by tourists such as the Rainbow Street area, known for its cafes and vibrant atmosphere. However, even in the capital, dressing modestly is recommended to avoid unwanted attention.

In contrast, rural areas and smaller towns tend to be more conservative. When visiting places like Madaba, known for its ancient mosaics, or the Dana Biosphere Reserve, it is especially important to adhere to modest dress codes. The same applies to cultural and historical sites like Petra and Jerash, where tourists should show respect for local customs despite the large influx of international visitors.

Beaches and Resorts

At the Dead Sea and Aqaba, where there are popular beach resorts, the dress code can be more relaxed within the confines of private hotel beaches and pools. However, it is respectful to cover up when moving away from these areas. Bikinis and swimsuits are acceptable at private beaches, but outside these areas, more conservative swimwear is advisable.

Dead Sea Marriott Resort & Spa: This resort offers a private beach area where swimwear is acceptable. However, it is advisable to wear a cover-up when leaving the beach area.

Kempinski Hotel Aqaba Red Sea: Located at the Red Sea, this luxury resort has a private beach where Western swimwear is the norm. Respect local customs by covering up when moving through public spaces within the resort.

Business and Social Settings
For business meetings or formal social gatherings, Jordanians generally dress conservatively. Men should wear suits or at least smart trousers with a long-sleeved shirt, while women should opt for business attire that covers their arms and legs. Understanding these nuances can help in making a good impression in professional and social settings.

Public Behavior and Etiquette
Beyond dress code, understanding public behavior and etiquette is also crucial. Public displays of affection are frowned upon, and it's advisable to avoid any behavior that could be seen as disrespectful. Politeness and hospitality are highly valued, and Jordanians often greet each other with a handshake. However, men should wait for a woman to extend her hand first.

Practical Tips
Carry a Scarf: Women should carry a scarf at all times for unexpected visits to religious sites.

Respect Local Customs: Dressing modestly shows respect for local traditions and can enhance your experience.

Observe Others: When in doubt, observe how locals are dressed and follow suit.

Religious Practices and Respectful Behavior

Understanding Islam in Jordan
Islam is the predominant religion in Jordan, with over 90% of the population identifying as Sunni Muslim. The remaining population includes Christians and small communities of other faiths. The practice of Islam in Jordan is moderate, but certain traditions and practices are strictly followed. Understanding the basics of Islam can help you navigate social interactions and public spaces respectfully.

Daily Prayers (Salat)
Muslims perform five daily prayers, known as Salat, which are observed at specific times throughout the day: Fajr (pre-dawn), Dhuhr (midday), Asr (afternoon), Maghrib (sunset), and Isha (evening). During prayer times, you will hear the call to prayer (Adhan) from mosques, which is a significant part of the daily rhythm in Jordanian life.

While it is not expected for non-Muslims to participate in the prayers, it is important to be mindful and respectful. If you are in a public place or visiting a mosque during prayer times, try to remain quiet and avoid interrupting those who are praying. In some areas, businesses may temporarily close or reduce their activity during prayers.

Visiting Mosques
Visiting mosques can be a highlight of your trip, offering a glimpse into the spiritual and architectural heritage of Jordan. However, there are specific rules you must follow to show respect:

Dress Modestly: Men should wear long pants and avoid sleeveless shirts. Women should cover their heads with a scarf and wear long skirts or pants and long-sleeved tops. Many mosques provide scarves and robes for visitors.

Remove Shoes: It is customary to remove your shoes before entering a mosque. There are usually designated areas to leave your shoes at the entrance.

Respect Prayer Areas: Avoid walking in front of people who are praying. In larger mosques, there might be designated areas for tourists; stay within these areas to avoid disturbing worshippers.

Photography: Always ask for permission before taking photos inside a mosque. Some mosques may have restrictions on photography, especially during prayer times.

Ramadan
Ramadan is the holy month of fasting, observed by Muslims worldwide. During Ramadan, Muslims fast from dawn to sunset, refraining from eating, drinking, smoking, and other physical needs. The dates for Ramadan vary each year based on the lunar calendar.
If you visit Jordan during Ramadan, you will notice changes in daily routines and business hours. Restaurants may be closed during the day and open only after sunset for Iftar, the meal that breaks the fast. It is respectful to avoid eating, drinking, or smoking in public during fasting hours. Many hotels and restaurants will have designated areas where non-Muslims can eat and drink during the day.

Dress Code
Jordan is a conservative country, and dressing modestly is important to show respect for local customs. While major cities like Amman may have a more relaxed dress code, it is still advisable to dress conservatively, especially in rural areas and religious sites.

Men: Avoid wearing shorts and sleeveless shirts in public. Long pants and short or long-sleeved shirts are appropriate.

Women: Shoulders, knees, and cleavage should be covered. Loose-fitting clothing is preferable. In some areas, especially in the south, women may feel more comfortable wearing a headscarf, although it is not mandatory.

Social Etiquette

Jordanian culture places a strong emphasis on hospitality and respect. Here are some key points to keep in mind:

Greetings: A common greeting is "As-salamu alaykum" (peace be upon you), to which the response is "Wa alaykum as-salam" (and peace be upon you). Handshakes are common among men, but for men greeting women, it is best to wait for the woman to extend her hand first. If she does not, a slight nod and smile will suffice.

Gestures: Avoid using your left hand for eating or handing over items, as it is considered unclean. The right hand is used for these actions.

Respecting Elders: Show respect to elders by standing when they enter a room and allowing them to speak first. It is also polite to address them with appropriate titles, such as "Haj" or "Hajja" for those who have completed the pilgrimage to Mecca.

Visiting Homes: If you are invited to a Jordanian home, it is customary to bring a small gift, such as sweets or flowers. Remove your shoes before entering and follow your host's lead in terms of seating and dining etiquette.

Public Displays of Affection: Public displays of affection between men and women are frowned upon. It is best to avoid kissing, hugging, or holding hands in public.

Dining Etiquette

Jordanian cuisine is rich and diverse, with meals often being a social event shared with family and friends. When dining, observe the following etiquette:

Sharing Food: Meals are often served family-style, with everyone sharing from common dishes. Use your right hand to take food and avoid reaching across the table.

Tea and Coffee: Offering tea or coffee is a sign of hospitality. Accepting a cup, even if you only take a sip, is polite. If you do not want a refill, gently shake your cup side to side.

Compliments and Conversations: It is customary to compliment the food and show appreciation to your host. Engaging in light conversation during the meal is common, but avoid topics like politics or religion unless brought up by your host.

Respect for Cultural Heritage
Jordan is home to numerous historical and cultural sites, from the ancient city of Petra to the Roman ruins of Jerash. When visiting these sites, it is crucial to show respect for the cultural heritage:

Do Not Touch Artifacts: Many sites have ancient artifacts that are fragile. Avoid touching or climbing on these structures to preserve them for future generations.

Stay on Marked Paths: Follow the designated paths and signs to avoid damaging the site and for your own safety.

Respect Local Guides: Local guides have extensive knowledge and a deep connection to the heritage sites. Listen to their instructions and ask questions to learn more about the history and culture.

Chapter 10:

Accommodation Options

Hotels and Resorts

The Ritz-Carlton, Amman

Located in the heart of Amman, The Ritz-Carlton combines luxury with impeccable service. This five-star hotel is situated at **Said Al-Mufti Street, Shmeisani, Amman 11183**. It features spacious rooms with panoramic city views, an extensive spa, and a variety of dining options. The Ritz-Carlton is known for its sophisticated design and exceptional customer service. The hotel's restaurants offer diverse menus, including international and local cuisine. The Ritz-Carlton's facilities also include a fitness center, indoor pool, and business services.

Sheraton Amman Al Nabil Hotel

Positioned at **5th Circle, Amman 11183**, the Sheraton Amman Al Nabil Hotel provides a blend of luxury and comfort. The hotel features elegantly decorated rooms, an outdoor pool, and a well-equipped fitness center. Its dining options include a range of international cuisines, and the hotel's location makes it a convenient base for exploring the city. Guests can enjoy the hotel's spa services and executive lounge, which provides additional amenities for business travelers.

Grand Millennium Amman

You'll find the Grand Millennium Amman at **Shemisani, Amman 11183**, offering contemporary luxury and excellent amenities. The hotel is well-suited for both business and leisure travelers, with spacious rooms, a rooftop pool, and a variety of dining options. The Grand Millennium also features a spa, fitness center, and business services, ensuring a comfortable and convenient stay in the capital.

Mövenpick Resort Petra

Located directly at the entrance of Petra, **Wadi Musa, Petra**, the Mövenpick Resort Petra provides unparalleled access to the ancient city. The hotel features rooms designed in traditional Jordanian style, a variety of dining options, and an outdoor pool. The Mövenpick Resort Petra also offers a spa, fitness center, and a range of services designed to enhance your experience in the region. Its proximity to Petra makes it a prime choice for those wanting to explore the archaeological site.

Petra Marriott Hotel

Situated at **P.O. Box 2535, Wadi Musa, Petra**, the Petra Marriott Hotel provides comfortable accommodation with modern amenities. The hotel's rooms offer views of the surrounding mountains, and its facilities include a restaurant, outdoor pool, and fitness center. The Petra Marriott Hotel is well-regarded for its hospitality and is a good option for travelers seeking convenience and comfort near Petra.

Taybet Zaman Hotel

For a more traditional experience, the Taybet Zaman Hotel, located at **Wadi Musa, Petra**, offers a unique stay. This hotel is designed to reflect traditional Jordanian architecture and culture. It features charming rooms, a swimming pool, and a restaurant serving local cuisine. The Taybet Zaman Hotel provides a serene atmosphere and is ideal for travelers looking for an authentic Jordanian experience.

Kempinski Hotel Ishtar Dead Sea

The Kempinski Hotel Ishtar is a luxurious retreat located at **Dead Sea Road, Sweimah, Jordan**. This five-star resort offers direct access to the Dead Sea, allowing you to enjoy its therapeutic waters and mud. The hotel features opulent rooms with sea views, multiple swimming pools, a world-class spa, and several dining options. The Kempinski is known for its high-end amenities and exceptional service, making it a premier choice for relaxation and luxury.

Marriott Dead Sea Resort & Spa

Located at **Dead Sea Road, Sweimah, Jordan**, the Marriott Dead Sea Resort & Spa provides a blend of luxury and relaxation. This resort features a range of facilities, including a large outdoor pool, spa services, and various dining options. The Marriott Dead Sea Resort is renowned for its extensive spa treatments and stunning views of the Dead Sea. It is an excellent choice for travelers seeking comfort and leisure.

Hilton Dead Sea Resort & Spa

The Hilton Dead Sea Resort & Spa, situated at **Dead Sea Road, Sweimah, Jordan**, offers a luxurious experience with direct access to the Dead Sea. The resort features spacious rooms, a private beach area, and an extensive spa. Guests can enjoy the resort's multiple dining venues, infinity pool, and fitness center. The Hilton Dead Sea Resort is ideal for those looking for a high-end stay with excellent facilities and beautiful views.

InterContinental Aqaba Resort
Located at **King Hussein Street, Aqaba**, the InterContinental Aqaba Resort offers luxury and convenience near the Red Sea. The resort features elegantly designed rooms, a private beach, and a range of dining options. It also includes a spa, outdoor pool, and fitness center. The InterContinental Aqaba is well-suited for both relaxation and exploration, providing easy access to local attractions and the vibrant city of Aqaba.

Hyatt Regency Aqaba Resort & Villas
You'll find the Hyatt Regency Aqaba Resort & Villas at **King Hussein Street, Aqaba**, providing a mix of luxury and comfort. This resort offers beautifully appointed rooms with sea views, an outdoor pool, and a private beach area. The Hyatt Regency also features several dining options and a full-service spa, making it an excellent choice for both relaxation and adventure.

Movenpick Resort & Residences Aqaba
Situated at **Aqaba, Jordan**, the Movenpick Resort & Residences offers a blend of modern luxury and comfort. This resort provides spacious accommodations, a private beach, and an outdoor pool. Its facilities include a range of dining options, a spa, and a fitness center. The Movenpick Resort & Residences is ideal for families and couples alike, offering a relaxing and enjoyable stay by the Red Sea.

Sun City Camp

Located within Wadi Rum's protected area, **Sun City Camp** offers a unique desert experience. The camp features traditional Bedouin-style tents equipped with modern amenities. Guests can enjoy guided tours of the desert, camel rides, and stargazing. The camp provides a comfortable and immersive way to experience the beauty of Wadi Rum.

Basha's Camp

Basha's Camp, situated in the heart of Wadi Rum, offers a more traditional Bedouin experience. The camp features comfortable tents with basic amenities and provides a range of activities, including jeep tours and hiking. The camp's location allows for breathtaking views of the desert landscape and is a great choice for those looking to explore Wadi Rum's natural beauty.

Wadi Rum Night Luxury Camp

For a more upscale desert experience, the Wadi Rum Night Luxury Camp offers deluxe tents with private bathrooms and high-end furnishings. Located in Wadi Rum's stunning desert, the camp provides guided tours, camel rides, and traditional Bedouin meals. It is an excellent choice for travelers seeking comfort while experiencing the desert's unique environment.

Bedouin Camps in Wadi Rum

Choosing a Bedouin Camp

Bedouin camps in Wadi Rum range from basic to luxurious, each offering its own unique experience. When choosing a camp, consider what type of experience you want. Some camps offer traditional Bedouin hospitality with simple, comfortable accommodations, while others provide more upscale amenities.

Martian Campsite Located in the heart of Wadi Rum, Martian Campsite is renowned for its blend of traditional and modern comforts. The camp features spacious, well-decorated tents with private bathrooms, air conditioning, and panoramic desert views. The camp's restaurant serves authentic Bedouin cuisine, and guests can enjoy activities such as camel rides, jeep tours, and stargazing.
Address: Martian Campsite, Wadi Rum Village, Wadi Rum, Jordan
Contact: +962 7 9820 3132
Opening Hours: Open year-round; check with the camp for specific booking times and seasonal availability.

Sun City Camp Sun City Camp offers a more luxurious desert experience. It features deluxe tents with en-suite bathrooms and private terraces. The camp's common areas include a cozy lounge and a restaurant that serves a range of international and traditional dishes. Activities include guided tours of Wadi Rum, stargazing, and traditional Bedouin dance performances.
Address: Sun City Camp, Wadi Rum, Jordan
Contact: +962 7 9527 1172
Opening Hours: Open throughout the year; advanced booking is recommended.

Rahayeb Desert Camp Rahayeb Desert Camp combines comfort with authenticity. The camp offers standard and deluxe tents, with options for both shared and private facilities. Rahayeb Desert Camp is known for its friendly staff and immersive cultural experiences, including Bedouin music performances and traditional meals prepared in a communal style.
Address: Rahayeb Desert Camp, Wadi Rum, Jordan
Contact: +962 7 9112 2231
Opening Hours: Open year-round; reservations are advisable to secure a spot.

Bedouin Camp Experience

Staying in a Bedouin camp provides a glimpse into the traditional lifestyle of the Bedouin people. Here's what you can expect during your stay:

Accommodation Tents are typically spacious and furnished with beds, rugs, and low tables. Most camps provide basic amenities such as bedding, towels, and sometimes electricity. Deluxe camps offer more comfort, with en-suite bathrooms and air conditioning. Be prepared for varying levels of luxury depending on the camp you choose.

Meals Meals at Bedouin camps are an integral part of the experience. Traditional Bedouin cuisine often includes dishes like mansaf (lamb cooked with rice and yogurt), kabsa (spiced rice with meat), and fresh bread baked in a traditional clay oven. Meals are usually served in a communal dining area, allowing you to experience Bedouin hospitality firsthand.

Activities Bedouin camps in Wadi Rum offer a range of activities to enhance your desert experience. Popular activities include:

Jeep Tours: Explore the vast landscapes of Wadi Rum in a 4x4 vehicle, guided by local drivers who know the area intimately.

Camel Rides: Experience the desert at a slower pace with a camel ride, an iconic way to traverse the sandy dunes and rocky terrain.

Stargazing: The clear desert skies offer some of the best stargazing opportunities. Many camps provide telescopes and organized stargazing sessions.

Hiking: For those who prefer to explore on foot, there are several trails that offer stunning views of the desert landscape.

Cultural Etiquette
When staying at a Bedouin camp, it's important to respect local customs and traditions:

Dress Modestly: In line with local customs, wear modest clothing that covers your shoulders and knees. This is especially important when visiting cultural sites and interacting with local communities.

Respect Local Customs: Be mindful of Bedouin traditions, such as removing your shoes before entering communal areas and refraining from loud behavior.

Ask Before Taking Photos: While the desert landscape is a popular subject for photography, always ask for permission before photographing people, especially in more remote areas.

Booking Your Stay

Booking a Bedouin camp in Wadi Rum can be done directly through the camp's website, via phone, or through various online travel agencies. It is advisable to book well in advance, especially during peak travel seasons, to ensure availability and secure the best rates.

Tips for Booking:

Check Reviews: Look for recent reviews from other travelers to gauge the quality of the camp and the experiences offered.

Verify Inclusions: Ensure that the cost of your stay includes meals and activities if these are important to you.

Confirm Transportation: Many camps offer pickup and drop-off services from Wadi Rum Village or nearby towns. Confirm these arrangements when booking.

Guesthouses and Budget Stays

The Jordan Tower Hotel

Located in the heart of Amman's downtown, The Jordan Tower Hotel is a popular choice for budget travelers. This guesthouse is situated at 11 Al-Rainbow Street, Amman. The hotel offers basic yet comfortable rooms with free Wi-Fi and breakfast included. Its central location allows you to easily explore nearby attractions such as the Roman Theater and the Citadel. The hotel's friendly staff can provide valuable tips on local dining and sightseeing.

Beity Hotel
Found at 4th Circle, Al-Jubeiha, Amman, Beity Hotel offers an affordable stay with clean, simple rooms and a homey atmosphere. The hotel is close to the University of Jordan, making it a suitable option for visitors interested in the academic environment of the city. Beity Hotel provides free Wi-Fi and breakfast, with a restaurant on-site serving traditional Jordanian cuisine.

Bedouin Garden Village
Situated in Wadi Musa, just a short drive from Petra, Bedouin Garden Village offers budget travelers a unique experience. Located at Ma'in Hot Springs, Wadi Musa, the guesthouse features basic accommodations with an authentic Bedouin touch. This is an ideal base for exploring Petra, and the guesthouse also offers organized tours and cultural activities, including traditional Bedouin dinners.

Petra Bedouin Guesthouse
Positioned close to the Petra Visitor Center, Petra Bedouin Guesthouse is at Petra Street, Wadi Musa. The guesthouse offers simple, clean rooms with essential amenities. It is renowned for its welcoming atmosphere and helpful staff. The guesthouse serves a hearty breakfast, and you can also enjoy traditional Jordanian meals in the evening. Its proximity to Petra

makes it a convenient choice for early morning explorations of the archaeological site.

The Seven Wonders Hotel
Located at Ma'in, Wadi Musa, The Seven Wonders Hotel is a budget-friendly option offering comfortable rooms with free Wi-Fi. This hotel provides easy access to Petra and is known for its friendly staff and clean facilities. The on-site restaurant serves a variety of dishes, and the hotel can assist in arranging tours and activities in the Petra area.

Wadi Rum Bedouin Camp
For a truly immersive experience, the Wadi Rum Bedouin Camp provides a traditional desert stay. Located in Wadi Rum Village, the camp offers basic yet comfortable tents with stunning views of the surrounding desert landscape. The camp's communal dining area serves traditional Jordanian meals, and you can enjoy activities like camel rides and jeep tours organized by the camp.

Rummana Campsite
Situated in the heart of Wadi Rum, Rummana Campsite provides budget-friendly tent accommodations with essential amenities. Located at Wadi Rum, this campsite offers a chance to experience the desert environment up close. The campsite includes breakfast and dinner, with options to join guided tours and desert activities.

Kempinski Hotel Aqaba
While primarily a luxury hotel, Kempinski offers occasional budget-friendly promotions that can be an excellent option for

travelers looking for a bit more comfort without spending excessively. Located at the Red Sea waterfront, it's a short distance from the city center and provides beautiful views, a private beach, and a variety of dining options.

Cedar Hotel
Located at 33 King Hussein Street, Aqaba, Cedar Hotel is a practical choice for budget travelers. The hotel offers straightforward rooms with basic amenities and is within walking distance of Aqaba's central attractions, including the beach and local markets.

Cedar Hotel provides a complimentary breakfast and has a small on-site restaurant.

Madaba Hotel
Positioned at 23 King Hussein Street, Madaba, this hotel offers affordable accommodations with a convenient location for exploring the nearby historical sites. The rooms are simple and clean, with free Wi-Fi and breakfast. The hotel's proximity to attractions like the Madaba Mosaic Map makes it an ideal base for visitors interested in the region's history.

Queen Ayola Hotel
Located at 2nd Circle, Madaba, Queen Ayola Hotel offers budget-friendly rooms with essential amenities. The hotel is known for its welcoming staff and convenient location near Madaba's historical sites. The restaurant on-site serves local dishes, and the hotel can assist with arranging local tours.

Jerash Village Hotel

Found at Jerash City Center, this hotel offers affordable and comfortable rooms with free Wi-Fi. Its central location makes it easy to explore the nearby Roman ruins of Jerash. The hotel provides a simple breakfast and has a restaurant serving local cuisine.

Dead Sea Bedouin Camp
For those visiting the Dead Sea, the Dead Sea Bedouin Camp offers a budget-friendly way to experience the area. Located along the shores of the Dead Sea, the camp provides basic tent accommodations with access to the mineral-rich waters. You can enjoy a traditional Jordanian meal at the camp and take part in various water activities.

Conclusion:

Final Tips on Traveling in Jordan

Understanding Jordanian Culture and Etiquette

Jordanian culture is deeply rooted in traditions and customs that reflect the country's Bedouin heritage and Islamic values. Respect for local customs and etiquette is crucial for a positive experience. When interacting with locals, dress modestly. For both men and women, covering shoulders and knees is appreciated, especially when visiting religious sites. Greetings are often warm and involve shaking hands, though women should wait for men to initiate a handshake. Always ask for permission before taking photographs, particularly of people.

Language and Communication

While Arabic is the official language, English is widely spoken in tourist areas and major cities like Amman, Petra, and Aqaba. However, learning a few basic Arabic phrases can enhance your interactions and show respect for the local culture. Simple greetings such as "Marhaban" (Hello) and "Shukran" (Thank you) can go a long way.

Transportation and Getting Around

Jordan's transportation network is quite accessible for tourists. In Amman, you can use taxis or ride-sharing services like Uber and Careem for convenient travel. For longer distances, such as between Amman and Petra, or Aqaba, consider renting a car. Rental agencies are available in major cities and at airports. Keep in mind that driving in Jordan follows a right-hand system, and road signs are often in both Arabic and English.

Safety and Health
Jordan is generally a safe destination for tourists. The country maintains a stable environment, though it is always wise to stay informed about the current situation. When it comes to health, tap water in urban areas is treated and generally safe to drink, but it's advisable to stick to bottled water in rural regions. Ensure you have travel insurance that covers health care and emergencies.

Currency and Payments
The Jordanian Dinar (JOD) is the local currency. Currency exchange services are available at airports, hotels, and banks. Credit and debit cards are widely accepted in major establishments, but it's a good idea to carry some cash for smaller shops or rural areas. Be mindful of currency exchange rates and fees, which can vary.

Local Cuisine and Dining
Jordanian cuisine is a highlight of any visit. Don't miss the opportunity to try traditional dishes such as Mansaf, a lamb dish cooked with yogurt and served with rice. Amman and other major cities have a variety of dining options, from high-end restaurants to local eateries. Some notable places include:

Hashem Restaurant, located at King Hussein Street, Amman, known for its falafel and hummus.

Fakhr El-Din, situated at 1st Circle, Amman, which offers an upscale dining experience with traditional Jordanian dishes.

The Royal Automobile Museum Café, found in King Hussein Park, Amman, ideal for a relaxed meal in a culturally rich setting.

Accommodations
Jordan offers a wide range of accommodations to suit different preferences and budgets. In Amman, you'll find luxury hotels such as the **Four Seasons Hotel**, located on Al Khushman Street, and **The Ritz-Carlton**, at 3rd Circle. For a more traditional experience, consider staying in a Bedouin camp in Wadi Rum, where you can experience authentic desert hospitality.

Cultural Sites and Attractions
Jordan is home to numerous world-renowned attractions. When visiting Petra, ensure you explore beyond the iconic Treasury and include the Monastery and High Place of Sacrifice. In Wadi Rum, consider taking a jeep tour to fully appreciate the desert's stunning landscapes. Dead Sea resorts, like the **Mövenpick Resort & Spa**, located on the shores of the Dead Sea, offer unique floating experiences due to the high salinity of the water.

Respect for Local Customs
As a visitor, it's essential to respect local customs and practices. When visiting religious sites, such as the Al-Hussein Mosque in Amman or the Baptism Site of Jesus Christ, dress conservatively and follow local guidelines. Always remove your

shoes before entering a mosque, and keep noise levels low in these sacred spaces.

Sustainability and Responsible Tourism
Jordan is committed to sustainable tourism practices. Support local conservation efforts by choosing eco-friendly tours and accommodations. Participate in initiatives that benefit local communities, such as buying handcrafted goods from local artisans or supporting projects that promote environmental preservation.

Encouragement to Visit Less Explored Regions

The Northern Highlands
In the northern part of Jordan, Ajloun presents a serene alternative to the country's more famous destinations. Ajloun Castle, perched on a hilltop, offers panoramic views of the surrounding countryside and the Jordan Valley. Built in the 12th century by the Ayyubids, the castle played a crucial role in defending the region from the Crusaders. Today, it's a fascinating historical site that provides insights into medieval military architecture and regional history. The castle is located in Ajloun Forest Reserve, which is also worth exploring for its beautiful walking trails and diverse flora and fauna.

Irbid
Nearby, Irbid, often overlooked by tourists, boasts significant historical and archaeological sites. The city is home to the ruins of Gadara, an ancient Greco-Roman city known for its well-

preserved theaters, baths, and mosaics. Wandering through the ancient streets of Gadara provides a sense of the grandeur that once characterized this region. Irbid itself is a lively university town with a rich cultural scene and vibrant local markets.

The Southern Desert

While Petra attracts most of the attention in southern Jordan, the nearby town of Ma'an offers a different perspective on the region. Ma'an is known for its historical significance and its role as a crossroads for trade and migration in ancient times. The Ma'an Archaeological Museum features artifacts from various periods, including the Nabataean and Roman eras. Exploring Ma'an allows you to appreciate the historical depth of the area beyond Petra's immediate fame.

Petra's Surroundings

Exploring beyond Petra's main archaeological site reveals lesser-known but equally intriguing attractions. The nearby town of Wadi Musa, often used as a base for visiting Petra, offers additional experiences such as local markets and traditional cuisine. For a more off-the-beaten-path adventure, consider a trek to Little Petra (Siq al-Barid), which is smaller but still impressive, showcasing Nabataean rock-cut architecture in a more tranquil setting.

The Jordan Valley

Located on the banks of the Jordan River, the Baptism Site (Bethany Beyond the Jordan) is a UNESCO World Heritage site with significant religious importance. This area is believed to be the location where John the Baptist baptized Jesus. Visiting this site offers a profound spiritual experience and a glimpse into the area's historical significance. The site includes various archaeological remains, including ancient churches and baptismal pools.

Natural Reserves

Jordan's natural reserves, such as the Dana Biosphere Reserve and the Mujib Nature Reserve, offer a stark contrast to the more famous sites. Dana Biosphere Reserve, with its diverse ecosystems ranging from rugged mountains to fertile valleys, provides ample opportunities for hiking and bird-watching. Mujib Nature Reserve, known for its dramatic landscapes and the Mujib River, offers exciting outdoor activities like canyoning and eco-tourism experiences. Both reserves are ideal for those looking to immerse themselves in Jordan's natural beauty and engage in sustainable travel practices.

The Eastern Desert

In the eastern part of Jordan, the Azraq Wetland Reserve presents an entirely different landscape from the arid desert commonly associated with the region. This oasis, which supports a variety of bird species and other wildlife, is crucial for the ecological balance of the area. The reserve includes several walking trails and observation points, making it a rewarding destination for nature enthusiasts. Additionally, the nearby Azraq Castle, a historical site with origins dating back to the Roman period, adds a historical dimension to the visit.

The Surrounding Desert

Exploring the eastern desert areas, including the ancient caravanserai at Qasr al-Kharana and Qasr Amra, reveals the architectural and cultural history of Jordan's desert regions. These structures, built during the Umayyad period, were used as rest stops along ancient trade routes and are known for their well-preserved frescoes and unique architectural features. Visiting these sites offers insights into the historical significance of the desert in regional trade and culture.

The Western Highlands

Madaba, often known as the "City of Mosaics," is famous for its Byzantine and Umayyad mosaics. The most notable of these is the Madaba Map, a mosaic floor map of the Holy Land that dates back to the 6th century. The town also features several other historical and religious sites, including St. George's Church and the Archaeological Park. Madaba's local market offers traditional crafts and foods, adding a cultural dimension to your visit.

Mount Nebo

Mount Nebo, located near Madaba, is traditionally believed to be the place where Moses viewed the Promised Land before his death. The summit provides breathtaking views of the Jordan Valley, the Dead Sea, and even Jerusalem on clear days. The site includes a modern church and various archaeological remains, making it a significant location for both historical and spiritual exploration.

Made in the USA
Las Vegas, NV
05 December 2024

13446590R00105